THE UPD
CAYMAN ISLAN
GUIDE

A FIRST-TIMER'S ESSENTIAL TIPS AND ITINERARY FOR EXPLORING THE VEILED GEMS, CUISINES, AND ICONIC LANDMARKS IN GRAND CAYMAN, CAYMAN BRAC, AND LITTLE CAYMAN

CHRISTINE M. EDMONSON

ACKNOWLEDGEMENT

I would like to convey my greatest thanks to everyone who contributed to the publication of "The Updated Cayman Island Travel Guide". Without your assistance, skill, and effort, this book would not have been possible.

First and foremost, I want to thank the people of the Cayman Islands for their warm hospitality, rich culture, and spectacular natural beauty. Your warmth and openness have left an indelible impact on my heart, and I am glad for the chance to explore and share the marvels of your islands with the world.

I express my deepest thanks to my family and friends for their unfailing support, understanding, and patience during the writing process. Your belief in me and your persistent support has been essential.

A particular thank you goes to the crew for their professionalism, direction, and experience in bringing this book to life. Your passion for quality is visible in every element of the guide.

I am thankful to the experts, residents, and travel professionals who freely provided their expertise, ideas, and suggestions. Your knowledge and enthusiasm have expanded the content of this book, providing readers with a complete and genuine resource.

Lastly, I would like to thank the readers of "The Updated Cayman Island Travel Guide" for their interest and support.
Your passion for experiencing the Cayman Islands and your love for travel drives me to continue developing excellent tools for travelers like you.

Please note that although every effort has been taken to guarantee the authenticity and dependability of the material contained in this book, travel circumstances and rules might change.

Once again, thank you, everybody, for being a part of this great adventure. Your contributions have made this book a reality, and I am thankful beyond words.

Christine M. Edmonson

CAYMAN ISLANDS
TRAVEL
Check List

Important Document

- Passport
- Identification
- Travel Tickets
- Travel documents
- Money : cash / credit cards / traveler's checks
- Vaccination Record
- Important Contact
- Travel guide / Maps
- Hotel Reservation

Clothing

- Shirts
- Pants
- Travel Tickets
- Swimwear
- Sweaters
- Soks

Toiletries

- Soap
- Shampoo
- Toothpaste
- Toothbrush
- Towel
- Sunscreen
- Deodorant
- Floss
- Perfume

Vacation Accessories

- Sunglasses
- Beach towels
- Travel Pillow
- Earplugs
- Tote bag
- Packing Cubes

TABLE OF CONTENTS

ACKNOWLEDGEMENT 3
TABLE OF CONTENTS 5
HOW TO USE THIS GUIDE 9

WELCOME TO THE CAYMAN ISLANDS 11
INTRODUCTION TO THE CAYMAN ISLANDS 13
History and Geography of the Cayman Islands 13
The Underrated Culture and Customs 17
Cayman Islands Language 24
Population and Population Demographics 24
Weather and Climate 25
Average temperatures 26
Rainfall 26
Best Time to Visit 27

Chapter 1 30
Travel Essentials and Tips 30
Visa Requirements and Entry Procedures 31
Visa Categories and Eligibility 34
Visa Application Process 35
Visa Application Fee 36
Travel Insurance 36
Flight Options and Estimated Cost 37
Money & Currency Exchange 39
Communication and Internet Access 41
Travel Cost and Budget 42
Estimated Budget for Solo Traveler 43
Affordable Choices for Couple 43
Budget Choices for a Family of Four 44

Chapter 2 45
MUSEUMS AND ART GALLERIES 45
Historical Sites and Landmarks 54
Cultural Festivals and Events 66
Annual Festivals and Celebrations 66
Music Festivals 68
Sporting Events and Competitions 70

Chapter 3 73
EXPLORING GRAND CAYMAN 73
Introduction to Grand Cayman 74
George Town: The Capital City 74
Seven Mile Beach: Sun, Sand, and Fun 75
Cayman Turtle Centre: A Sea Turtle Experience 78
Stingray City: Swimming with Friendly Rays 82
Pedro St. James National Historic Site: The
Birthplace of Democracy 85

Chapter 4 88
UNCOVERING CAYMAN BRAC 88
Introduction to Cayman Brac 89
Brac Reef Beach 90
The Bluff: Spectacular Views and Hiking Trails 93
Dive Sites and Snorkeling Spots 95
Rock Iguanas Sanctuary 101

Chapter 5 104
DISCOVERING LITTLE CAYMAN 104
Introduction to Little Cayman 105
Booby Pond Nature Reserve: Bird-watching Haven ..106
Point of Sand Beach: Secluded Paradise 108
Bloody Bay Marine Park: Underwater Wonders 112

Owen Island: A Hidden Gem 114

Chapter 6 117
CAYMANIAN DINING AND NIGHTLIFE 117
Caymanian Cuisine and Local Delicacies 119
Vegetarian and Vegan Options 121
Seafood Specialties 123
Fine Dining and Gourmet Experiences 124
Local Restaurants and Street Food 129
Beach Bars and Nightlife Hotspots 133

Chapter 7 143
SHOPPING AND SOUVENIRS 143
Duty-Free Shopping 144
Local Art and Craft Markets 149
Rare Souvenirs to Bring Home 154

Chapter 8 156
OUTDOOR ADVENTURES AND WATERSPORTS 156
Scuba Diving and Snorkeling 157
Sailing and Boating 158
Kayaking and Paddle-boarding 159
Fishing Excursions 160
Eco-Tours and Nature Walks 161
Caving and Exploration 162
Cycling and Hiking Trails 163
Golfing and Tennis Facilities 164
Rock Climbing and Rappelling 166
Beachcombing and Relaxation 167
Bird-watching 168
Sunset Cruises 169
Stargazing 170

Chapter 9 171

PRACTICAL INFORMATION 171

Transportation in the Cayman Islands 172

Accommodation Options 177

Luxury Resorts and Hotels 177

Boutique & Eco-Friendly Lodgings 181

Budget-Friendly Accommodations 186

Vacation Rentals and Villas 190

Camping and Outdoor Accommodations 194

Chapter 10 198

INSIDER TIPS & RECOMMENDATIONS 198

Local Customs and Etiquette 199

Safety Tips and Precautions 201

APPENDIX 203

7 Days Suggested Itinerary 204

Extra Health and Safety Information 207

Basic Phrases in Cayman Creole 209

Emergency Contacts 210

Downloadable & Printable Cayman Islands Maps 210

Packing List and Essentials 212

CONCLUSION 214

HOW TO USE THIS GUIDE

Welcome to the updated Cayman Islands Travel Guide! This extensive guide is meant to help you make the most of your visit to this great destination. Here's how you can effectively implement this guide:

Introduction: Begin by reading the introduction section to obtain a short sense of what to expect in the Cayman Islands and learn how this book is organized.

Preparing Your Trip: Start preparing your trip with the beneficial information supplied in this section. Discover the optimal time to go, understand admission requirements, and familiarize yourself with the local currency. Explore transportation options, and accommodation possibilities, and obtain essential packing tips.

Getting to Know the Cayman Islands: Dive into the heart of the Cayman Islands by understanding the history, culture, and natural beauty of the islands. Learn about local customs and etiquette to ensure a respectful and delightful stay.

Destination Highlights: Navigate through the unique sections dedicated to each island—Grand Cayman, Cayman Brac, and Little Cayman. Discover the must-visit attractions, iconic beaches, historical sites, and unique experiences that each island has to offer.

Outdoor Activities: If you're an adventure enthusiast, this region is for you. Find information on water sports, hiking pathways, bird-watching spots, golf courses, and adrenaline adventure activities available across the islands.

Dining and Nightlife: Indulge in the exciting culinary scene of the Cayman Islands. Discover traditional Caymanian cuisine, international restaurants, local food markets, and vibrant bars and nightclubs.

Don't miss out on attending cultural events and festivals for a sense of local culture.

Shopping and Souvenirs: Get insider's tips on where to uncover the greatest shopping deals, duty-free items, local handicrafts, and interesting souvenirs. Immerse yourself in the island's culture by seeing local markets and eating Caymanian delicacies.

Health and Safety: Prioritize your well-being by familiarizing yourself with the available medical services and facilities. Take note of emergency contacts and follow safety steps to insure a worry-free trip. Consider obtaining travel insurance for added peace of mind.

Practical Information: Find vital information on communication choices, local transportation, practical terminology, tipping customs, and a list of helpful contacts and websites.

Appendix: Utilize the appendix section for additional resources, including sample itineraries, and steps to download your maps.

WELCOME TO THE CAYMAN ISLANDS

Pack your bags and join the Henderson family as they escape the ordinary and head on a long-awaited vacation to the interesting Cayman Islands! After weeks of stressful school assignments and tough employment schedules, the Hendersons are ready to relax, refuel, and dig headfirst into the event of a lifetime!

As the flight touches down on the sun-kissed islands, a surge of adrenaline sweeps the air. With broad smiles and a bounce in their step, the Hendersons set foot on the sandy seashore, leaving behind the strain of everyday life. It's time to enjoy the gorgeous paradise that awaits them!

Days filled with pleasure, brightness, and endless adventure ahead. Picture the family swimming in the crystal-clear oceans, their spirits soaring as colorful fish dart around them. They bathe in the warm Caribbean sun on lovely beaches, making sandcastles and relishing in carefree moments of utter happiness.

From heart-pounding activity to tranquil rest, the Hendersons learn the genuine meaning of paradise. They zip-line through magnificent rainforests, their cries of joy bursting through the treetops. They eat beautiful local delicacies at bright beachside eateries, the flavors dancing on their tongues like a culinary symphony.

But it's not just about the activities they immerse themselves in the culture of the islands. They sway to the seductive strains of Caribbean music, joining locals in spontaneous dance parties under the starlit sky.

They listen intently to stories offered by the island's elders, seeking to learn the wisdom and rich history woven into the fabric of the Cayman Islands. With each passing day, the Hendersons feel the weight of their hectic lives falling away.

The issues and deadlines evaporate into insignificance as they reconnect with nature, themselves, and each other. They enjoy the simple pleasure of uninterrupted family time, establishing experiences that will be cherished for a lifetime.

As their vacation concludes, the Hendersons bid farewell to the Cayman Islands with a heavy heart. But they departed with a restored sense of peace, carrying the spirit of the islands within them. The memories of this amazing vacation will ignite their spirits as they dig back into the bustle of everyday life, motivating them to continuously seek moments of enjoyment and adventure.

Now, it's your opportunity to travel on your cruise to the Cayman Islands, just like the Hendersons did. Leave away the strain and routine, and let the charm of these lovely islands grip your soul. Get ready for unusual experiences, emotional interactions, and a vacation that will breathe new life into your exhausted spirit.

Don't forget to share your fantastic experiences and cherished memories with us, and stay tuned for more intriguing destinations and travel tales. Until then, pack your bags, follow your wanderlust, and let the journey unfold!

INTRODUCTION TO THE CAYMAN ISLANDS

The Cayman Islands is a British Overseas Territory situated in the western Caribbean Sea. The Cayman Islands are situated south of Cuba, northwest of Jamaica, and northeast of Honduras.

To the north and east, it is flanked by the Caribbean Sea. To the south, it is flanked by the Caribbean Sea and the Cayman Trench, which is one of the deepest areas of the Caribbean Sea. To the west, it is limited by the Yucatan Channel, which separates the islands from the Yucatan Peninsula of Mexico.

Please note that the angles of the Cayman Islands may change somewhat based on the particular reference point or mapping system used, but the coordinates supplied should give you a broad notion of the position.

History and Geography of the Cayman Islands

From the start of the 16th century to the dynamic present, the Cayman Islands have weaved a stunning tapestry of history, growing into the treasured destination we know today.

Long before the Cayman Islands became a desirable tourist destination, they were inhabited by the indigenous people known as the Taino and subsequently by the maritime cultures of the Caribs and Arawaks. However, it was Christopher Columbus who first set foot on the islands in 1503 during his last expedition to the New World.

The name "**Cayman**" is said to have derived from the Carib word "**caiman**," meaning "**crocodile**." These islands were previously populated by turtles and crocodiles, which Columbus met upon his arrival. Over time, the islands became a refuge for pirates and privateers who exploited the complex network of coves and secret caverns as their base of operations. Join us as we go on a trip through the past, examining the incredible events that have formed these islands.

16th-18th Centuries: The Cayman Islands first joined the historical scene in 1503, when Christopher Columbus saw the islands on his last trip to the New World. Named "Las Tortugas" because of the plentiful sea turtles he discovered, the islands were a favorite stopover for European explorers and privateers.

By the 17th century: the British Empire started extending its dominance over the area, culminating in the islands becoming a British Overseas Territory. The islands' strategic position attracted pirates, who exploited the concealed coves and caves to start their plundering exploits. Stories of renowned pirates like Blackbeard and Calico Jack have been handed down through generations, contributing to the mystery of the islands' past.

19th-20th Centuries: During the 19th century, the Cayman Islands saw a transformation in their economy. Shipbuilding and turtle fishing were key enterprises, providing livelihoods for the islanders. The sailors of the Cayman Islands were famous for their excellent boat-building talents, and their ships traversed the seas, transporting products and tales from faraway regions. **In the early 20th century**, the islands started opening up to tourists. Visitors were lured to the gorgeous beaches, vivid coral reefs, and kind hospitality. However, it was the advent of the financial services industry in the latter half of the 20th century that converted the Cayman Islands into a worldwide financial powerhouse. Today, the islands are recognized for their offshore banking, investment funds, and worldwide commercial services.

21st Century: Entering the 21st century, the Cayman Islands continued to develop, with an emphasis on sustainable tourism and maintaining its natural riches. The islands have become a sought-after destination for vacationers seeking a perfect balance of leisure and adventure.

The Cayman Islands have also been vigilant in conserving their maritime environments.

The development of marine parks, such as the famed Stingray City and Bloody Bay Marine Park, protects the preservation of coral reefs and the varied marine creatures that call them home.

Today: the Cayman Islands are recognized not just for their spectacular beauty but also for their kind and hospitable culture. Visitors may immerse themselves in local customs, experience gastronomic pleasures, and visit the islands' historical treasures, such as Pedro St. James Castle, the oldest stone edifice in the Cayman Islands.

As we stand at the threshold of this current century, the Cayman Islands continue to prosper as a destination that appreciates its history while looking toward the future.

With a dedication to sustainable development, maintaining their natural treasures, and delivering exceptional experiences, the islands remain a beacon of Caribbean beauty.

The Cayman Islands, situated in the western Caribbean Sea, comprise three major islands: Grand Cayman, Cayman Brac, and Little Cayman. Each island possesses its own distinct charm and natural beauty.

Grand Cayman, the biggest and most developed of the three, is a busy center of activity. Its stunning Seven Mile Beach, with its immaculate white sands and crystal-clear seas, is considered one of the world's most beautiful beaches. The island is also home to the bustling capital city of George Town, where you can explore historical monuments, engage in shopping, and sample local cuisine.

Cayman Brac, named for its distinctive limestone cliff ("brac" means "bluff" in Gaelic), provides a rough and adventurous experience.

The island is a delight for nature enthusiasts, with its lush woods, spectacular cliffs, and an abundance of caverns ready to be discovered. It is also a popular location for diving lovers, who may explore an underwater world teamed with colorful marine life.

Little Cayman, the smallest and most calm of the three islands, is a haven for individuals seeking privacy and tranquility. It is a sanctuary for birdwatchers, with its rich bird population, including the uncommon red-footed booby. The island's Bloody Bay Marine Park provides world-class diving possibilities, showing magnificent coral reefs and a myriad of marine animals.

The topography of the Cayman Islands is defined by its famed coral reefs, which make it a hotspot for divers and snorkelers alike. The beautiful underwater environment is a symphony of hues, with a multitude of coral formations, tropical fish, and even the possibility to meet stately sea turtles and gentle stingrays.

As you immerse yourself in the rich history and compelling landscape of the Cayman Islands, you will unearth a world where stories of pirates come to life, where nature thrives in its most beautiful forms, and where the appeal of turquoise seas and immaculate beaches begs you to explore.

So, my tourist, prepare to be captured by the beauty of the Cayman Islands. Step into a place where history whispers secrets from the past, where natural marvels leave you in amazement, and where the spirit of adventure awaits around every turn. Get ready to write your memorable narrative amid this paradise of sun, sea, and enthralling history.

The Underrated Culture and Customs

The culture of the Cayman Islands is a compelling combination of influences that reflects the rich background of its people. Rooted in the traditions of the early settlers and mixed with Caribbean, African, and European cultures, Caymanian culture is a tapestry of vivid festivities, culinary delights, music, and art. As you dive into the lesser-known facets of the islands' culture, expect to be fascinated by their distinct rituals and deep-rooted past.

Caymanian Hospitality: From the time you arrive, you'll be welcomed with kind grins and open arms, immediately feeling like part of the extended family. Caymanians are noted for their accessible manner, willing to offer their tales, customs, and insider advice to improve your visit.

The feeling of community in the Cayman Islands is apparent, where everyone is considered family. Locals take delight in sharing their expertise and customized suggestions, ensuring that you uncover the hidden jewels and experience the greatest local food.

Caymanian friendliness extends beyond surface-level encounters. Generosity and friendliness are essential qualities of Caymanian hospitality. Expect acts of kindness, from rescuing lost tourists to welcoming you into their homes for a home-cooked lunch. Caymanians appreciate and celebrate diversity, providing you the chance to meet with individuals from other origins and learn about their traditions.

The relationships created during your vacation have the potential to last for a lifetime. Stay in contact with the residents you've met, trade tales and images, and allow the relationships you've built to serve as a reminder of the warmth and friendliness that characterize Caymanian hospitality.

Culinary Delights: Caymanian cuisine is a wonderful combination of tastes that represents the islands' rich culture and traditions.

Influenced by African, Caribbean, British, and Jamaican traditions, the local cuisines delight the taste buds with a unique combination of spices, fresh fish, and locally obtained ingredients. Indulge in meals like conch fritters, fish rundown, and turtle stew, which emphasize the island's profound relationship to the water. Don't miss the traditional Caymanian Sunday breakfast, a delectable feast of fish, cassava cake, and hefty pastries. Experience the culinary legacy via varied tastes, and let the food lead you on a gourmet trip into the heart of Caymanian culture.

Music and Dance: Music plays a unique position in Caymanian culture, with styles like soca, reggae, and calypso filling the air. Join in the rhythmic rhythms of local musicians and experience the contagious energy of traditional dances, such as the famed "Quadrille." Celebrate at local festivals, where the sounds of steel pans and the swing of hips create an atmosphere of sheer delight.

Religious Observances: The Cayman Islands have a strong religious background, with Christianity being a major religion. The Church plays a large role in the community, and religious observances are recognized and treasured.

Seafaring Traditions: As a region integrally tied to the water, seafaring traditions retain tremendous importance in Caymanian culture. From boat construction to fishing practices handed down through generations, the nautical tradition is strongly established. Explore the intriguing history of shipwrecks and legends of pirates that have formed the island's mythology.

Art and Crafts: The creative expression of the Cayman Islands is present in different forms, including thatch weaving, woodcarving, and painting. Admire the meticulous workmanship of Caymanian artists as they produce magnificent items inspired by the natural beauty of the islands.

Preserving Natural Beauty: Caymanians strongly cherish their natural surroundings and actively participate in conservation initiatives to safeguard the pristine environment. The passion for the environment is obvious in the effort to maintain sensitive ecosystems, particularly the safeguarding of the famed Blue Iguana and the beautiful coral reefs that surround the islands.

Traditional attire: Caymanian traditional attire is a lively representation of the islands' rich culture and traditions. The Catboat Thatch and Bandana outfit stands out, with a thatch skirt and a headscarf crafted from the Silver Thatch Palm.
Admire the meticulous workmanship of Caymanian artists as they produce magnificent items inspired by the natural beauty of the islands.

Preserving Natural Beauty: Caymanians strongly cherish their natural surroundings and actively participate in conservation initiatives to safeguard the pristine environment. The passion for the environment is obvious in the effort to maintain sensitive ecosystems, particularly the safeguarding of the famed Blue Iguana and the beautiful coral reefs that surround the islands.

Traditional attire: Caymanian traditional attire is a lively representation of the islands' rich culture and traditions. The Catboat Thatch and Bandana outfit stands out, with a thatch skirt and a headscarf crafted from the Silver Thatch Palm.
Admire the delicate workmanship and historical importance of this outfit, reflecting the link to the land and sea. Beyond its aesthetic attractiveness, Caymanian traditional attire signifies a proud legacy and acts as a reminder of the islanders' tenacity and ingenuity.

Embrace the chance to learn about the cultural importance of wearing these costumes to immerse yourself in the traditions and tales woven into the fabric of the Cayman Islands.

Cultural Festivals: From colorful parades to rhythmic dances and traditional music, these festivities give a tantalizing peek into the heart of Caymanian culture.
These events not only amuse but also promote a better knowledge of Caymanian tradition, generating a feeling of solidarity and pride among natives and tourists alike.

Oral Traditions: The Cayman Islands have a significant heritage of oral storytelling. Beyond the well-known stories, explore lesser-known traditions and folklore that emphasize the island's relationship to the water, mystical animals, and the perseverance of the Caymanian people. Engage with locals, who are ready to share their tales and keep these narratives alive. Caymanian oral traditions pour life into the past, linking generations and sustaining the cultural uniqueness of these magnificent islands.

Heritage Homes: Step into the past by visiting the historic Caymanian dwellings, known as "wattle and daub" cottages. Caymanian historic houses are more than simply architectural wonders; they symbolize the rich culture and traditions of the islands. These historic dwellings represent the deep-rooted link between the Caymanian people and their heritage. Built with indigenous resources, such as limestone and thatch, these dwellings highlight the workmanship and ingenuity of prior generations. By maintaining and honoring historic residences, Caymanians commemorate their traditions, ensuring that future generations may connect with their vivid history and embrace their distinct cultural identity.

Caymanian Traditional Healing: Caymanian culture and traditions are strongly steeped in a long legacy of holistic healing methods.

From generation to generation, Caymanians have handed down their knowledge of natural medicines and herbal therapies.
Drawing upon the plentiful resources of the islands, these ancient healing methods harness the force of nature to promote well-being and restore balance.

Caymanian traditional medicine spans a broad variety of methods, from employing medicinal plants and herbs to combining rituals and spiritual beliefs. Local healers, known as "bush doctors," possess an intimate awareness of the island's plants and their medicinal abilities. They skillfully blend diverse herbs, roots, and other natural substances to develop cures that treat a broad diversity of diseases.

The medicines applied in Caymanian traditional healing are as varied as the island's nature. From aloe vera for mending sunburns to the moringa tree for its rich nutrients, the therapeutic power of these natural compounds is astonishing. Caymanian healers have polished their profession through years of observation and experimentation, retaining their traditional knowledge.

Beyond the physical components, traditional medicine in Caymanian culture stresses the significance of spiritual and emotional well-being. Rituals and scared practices are typically interwoven into the healing process to reestablish equilibrium between mind, body, and spirit. These practices are strongly based on the concept that genuine healing needs to address the whole essence of a person.

Cultural Preservation: The Cayman Islands attach high emphasis on conserving their cultural legacy.
Visit the National Museum and explore exhibitions that display the islands' history, artifacts, and tales.
Engage with cultural groups and attend events that promote traditional arts, crafts, and music.

Silver Thatch Palm: The Silver Thatch Palm carries enormous importance in Caymanian culture. This multipurpose tree is tightly intertwined into the fabric of Caymanian culture. Its fronds are masterfully turned into thatch roofs, providing a unique architectural style visible in many local structures. The Silver Thatch Palm also serves as a significant material for manufacturing traditional hats and baskets, showing the skill and workmanship of the Caymanian people. This cherished palm is not only a utilitarian resource but also a symbol of cultural history, linking generations and sustaining the distinctive rituals of the Cayman Islands

Moonlight Sailing: Caymanian Moonlight Sailing is an amazing cultural ritual that displays the profound connection between the people and the water. As the moon sheds its beautiful shine onto the peaceful waters, locals take a sail, led by its light. This age-old ritual inspires a feeling of tranquility, presenting a unique vision of the islands beneath the heavenly canopy.

Traditional Games: Caymanian culture and traditions come to life via their traditional games, allowing a look into the lively spirit of the islands. Engage in the thrill of "Marble Time," when individuals display their abilities in marble tournaments, encouraging friendly rivalry and togetherness. Experience the excitement of "Road Tennis," a local form of table tennis played on paved roads, merging athleticism and agility.

Blue Iguana Conservation: The Caymanian culture greatly values the preservation of its natural heritage, particularly the critically endangered Blue Iguana. As a cultural emblem and national treasure, the Caymanian community has pulled together to safeguard and restore the population of these amazing reptiles.

Conservation efforts, spearheaded by devoted people and groups, have successfully brought the Blue Iguana back from the verge of extinction.

This devotion to conservation is embedded into the fabric of Caymanian culture, with inhabitants actively engaging in projects, teaching tourists, and developing sustainable ecosystems.

Mementos from the water: Caymanian culture and traditions are strongly connected with the riches discovered in the water. From seashells and coral pieces to sea glass, craftsmen combine these natural beauties into magnificent memories that represent the soul of the islands. Admire the artistry of local artists as they produce unique jewelry and decorative objects, each piece reflecting a narrative of the sea's splendor.

These relics serve as physical reminders of the Cayman Islands' rich nautical past and the intimate link between the people and the water. Take home a piece of this valued culture and keep the spirit of the Cayman Islands alive in your heart.

Traditional Fishing Methods: Caymanian culture and traditions are strongly connected with the sea, and traditional fishing methods play a key part in their legacy. Passed down through generations, these skills show their ecological habits and intimate connection to the water.

Caymanian fishermen utilize a range of tactics, including hand-lining, fish traps, and the usage of "fish pots." Hand-lining includes utilizing a single fishing line with bait, requiring skill and patience to lure in the catch. Fish traps, known as "fish weirs," are ingeniously crafted structures that direct fish into a trap, assuring a rich harvest.

A distinctive characteristic of Caymanian fishing is the usage of "fish pots," which are submerged containers meant to attract and collect fish.

Crafted with care, these pots are deliberately positioned in the water, employing natural materials and skills handed down through generations.

These ancient fishing methods reflect the Caymanian dedication to sustainable practices and the preservation of marine resources. By utilizing practices that preserve the natural balance of the environment, Caymanians have maintained a healthy connection with the sea for millennia.

Cayman Islands Language

The official language of the Cayman Islands is English, making it easier for tourists to converse and explore the islands. English is spoken by the majority of the population and utilized in official government processes, commercial transactions, and educational institutions. The clarity and fluency of the English language in the Cayman Islands offer a seamless experience for tourists from English-speaking nations.

However, it is worth mentioning that you may also hear a distinct Caymanian dialect known as Caymanian Patois, or Cayman Creole.
This indigenous dialect contains aspects of African, Caribbean, and English languages, reflecting the rich cultural past of the islands. Embrace the chance to acquire a few local terms and expressions, as it may enrich your interactions and develop a stronger connection with the local community.

Population and Population Demographics

The Cayman Islands has a population of 67,967 as of June 2, 2023, according to the latest United Nations projections. This comparatively modest population number adds to the islands' intimate and close-knit communal vibe.

The population density is 274 persons per square kilometer. The bulk of the population is of West Indian heritage, with lesser groups of European, North American, and Asian descent. It is not commonplace to meet individuals from many origins including Caymanian, Jamaican, British, American, Canadian, and many more. The bulk of the population is on Grand Cayman, the biggest of the three islands, while Cayman Brac and Little Cayman have smaller populations.

The Cayman Islands is a British overseas territory that boasts a good quality of life. The economy is built on tourism, financial services, and offshore banking. Here are some more statistics regarding the Cayman Islands population:

1. The population is expanding at a pace of roughly 2% each year.
2. The median age is 37 years old.
3. The literacy rate is 99%.
4. The unemployment rate is 3.5%.
5. The life expectancy is 81 years.

Weather and Climate

The Cayman Islands have a tropical marine climate, with a wet season of warm, rainy summers (May–October) and a dry season of comparatively moderate winters (November to April).

Summer (May–October): Temperatures are warm and humid, with typical highs of 86°F (30°C) and lows of 77°F (25°C). There is an average of 12 inches of rain every month throughout this period.

Winter (November–April): Temperatures are colder and drier, with average highs of 82°F (28°C) and lows of 72°F (22°C). There is an average of 4 inches of rain every month throughout this period.

Average temperature

Here are the average temperatures in the Cayman Islands:

MONTH	LOW	HIGH
January	72°F (22°C)	82°F (28°C)
February	73°F (23°C)	83°F (28°C)
March	74°F (23°C)	84°F (29°C)
April	75°F (24°C)	85°F (30°C)
May	77°F (25°C)	86°F (30°C)
June	78°F (26°C)	87°F (31°C)
July	79°F (26°C)	88°F (31°C)
August	80°F (27°C)	89°F (32°C)
September	79°F (26°C)	88°F (31°C)
October	78°F (26°C)	87°F (31°C)
November	77°F (25°C)	86°F (30°C)
December	76°F (24°C)	85°F (29°C)

As you can see, the temperatures in the Cayman Islands are fairly warm year-round. The warmest months are July and August when the average high temperature is 89°F (32°C). The coldest months are December and January when the average high temperature is 82°F (28°C).

The Cayman Islands also have a very high humidity level, which may make the temperature seem even warmer. The humidity level is maximum during the summer months, when it may approach 90%.

Rainfall

The average annual rainfall in the Cayman Islands is 60 inches. The wettest month is September, with an average rainfall of 12 inches. The driest month is February, with an average rainfall of 2 inches.

Here is a table showing the average monthly rainfall in the Cayman Islands:

26

MONTH	Rainfall (inches)
January	2
February	2
March	3
April	4
May	6
June	7
July	8
August	9
September	12
October	10
November	6
December	4

As you can see, the Cayman Islands receive the most rainfall during the summer months. However, it is important to note that the Cayman Islands are a tropical destination and rain can occur at any time of year.

If you are planning a trip to the Cayman Islands, it is important to pack for all types of weather. Be sure to pack sunscreen, a hat, sunglasses, and a rain jacket. You may also want to pack some light clothing for the evenings, as the temperatures can drop slightly.

Best Time to Visit
I would suggest visiting the Cayman Islands during the shoulder seasons, which include the months of May, June, September, and October. The weather is still nice and sunny, but the people are less and the costs are cheaper.

Here are some of the reasons why I would suggest visiting the Cayman Islands during the shoulder seasons:

1. Weather: The weather is warm and sunny throughout these months, giving it a fantastic time to relax on the beach, go swimming, or go snorkeling or diving.

2. Crowds: The crowds are lower during the shoulder seasons, so you may enjoy the islands without having to battle the masses.

3. Activities: There are lots of things to do throughout the shoulder seasons, including swimming, sunbathing, snorkeling, diving, fishing, golfing, shopping, and experiencing the local culture.
However, based on weather and travel trends, these are the ideal times to visit the Cayman Islands.

The best time to visit the Cayman Islands is during the dry season, which normally spans from November to April. This season brings nice temperatures, decreased humidity levels, and less rainfall, making it excellent for outdoor activities and beach visits. The main tourist season is between December and April, so anticipate greater crowds and higher lodging fees during this period.

If you want a calmer and more budget-friendly experience, try going during the shoulder seasons of May to June and September to October. While there may be somewhat more odds of weather, the islands are still lovely, and you'll have more opportunities to explore without the crowds.

The summer months, from July through August, may be hot and humid, but they also provide fantastic chances for aquatic sports like snorkeling, diving, and swimming.

Just be prepared for intermittent rain showers and possibly hurricane activity, since the Cayman Islands are positioned in the Caribbean hurricane belt.

Ultimately, the ideal time to visit the Cayman Islands depends on your tastes, price, and availability. Each season has its particular attractions, and the islands are a pleasant trip year-round.

chapter one

Travel Essential Tips

Whether you're a first-time visitor or a seasoned traveler to the Cayman Islands, this chapter will provide you with the information you need to make the most of your journey.

In this chapter, I will cover everything from travel preparations and paperwork needs to insider advice on currency exchange, and communication. I'll also give tips on packing basics, and outfit suggestions for touring the islands.

Visa Requirements and Entry Procedures

When planning your vacation to the Cayman Islands, it's crucial to understand the visa requirements and entrance processes to guarantee a smooth and hassle-free voyage. Here's an outline of the visa requirements and admission processes for visiting the Cayman Islands:

Visa Exemptions

Many tourists visiting the Cayman Islands do not need a visa for visits up to 30 days.

This applies to inhabitants of nations such as the United States, Canada, the United Kingdom, European Union member states, Australia, New Zealand, and numerous more. Citizens of several nations, notably China, India, and Russia, do require a visa to visit the Cayman Islands. However, it's vital to examine the particular entrance criteria depending on your country, since exemptions might differ.

Passport Validity

Your passport should be valid for at least six months after your scheduled date of return from the Cayman Islands. If your passport is not valid for at least six months, you will not be able to enter the country.

When you apply for a passport, you will need to enter your date of birth, place of birth, and current address. You will also need to give a current passport-style image.

The application procedure might take several weeks, therefore it is crucial to apply for your passport well in advance of your departure date.

If you lose your passport while you are abroad, you should report it to the local police and the closest embassy or consulate in your home country. You will need to apply for a new passport before you may return home.

Here are some recommendations for keeping your passport secure when you are traveling:

1. Keep your passport in a safe location, such as a money belt or a secret pocket in your backpack.
2. Do not bring your passport with you while you are out and about.
3. Duplicate your passport and store it in a different location from your passport.
4. If you are going to a country where there is a danger of theft or violence, consider bringing a second form of identification, such as a driver's license or a national ID card.

Length of Stay
Visitors may normally remain in the Cayman Islands for 30- 90 days without a visa. If you want to remain longer, you may need to ask for an extension via the Immigration Department. It's crucial to stick to the specified period of your stay to prevent any legal difficulties.

Return Ticket and Proof of Accommodation
Upon arrival, immigration officials may require to see your return ticket or evidence of further travel. Ensure you have a confirmed return ticket or travel schedule that confirms your intention to depart the Cayman Islands within the authorized time range. Additionally, possessing documentation of lodging bookings for your stay might further expedite the immigration procedure.

Immigration Forms

Upon arriving in the Cayman Islands, you will be asked to complete immigration paperwork, including a customs declaration and an immigration arrival card. Fill out these forms carefully and honestly, supplying the required information asked.

COVID-19 Travel Requirements

Due to the continuing worldwide epidemic, extra health and safety precautions may be in place.

Check the current travel warnings and recommendations from the Cayman Islands Government or your local embassy to be updated about any COVID-19 testing, immunization, or quarantine requirements before and upon arrival.

It's essential to remember that visa requirements and entrance processes sometimes vary, so it's best to check the most up-to-date information from official sources such as the Cayman Islands Government or your local embassy before flying.

By familiarizing yourself with the visa requirements and entrance processes for the Cayman Islands, you can secure a smooth and hassle-free admission into this intriguing Caribbean location. Prepare your travel paperwork in advance, stick to the restrictions, and get ready to go on an amazing adventure to the lovely Cayman Islands.

Customs restrictions

You are permitted to bring in duty-free products for personal use, including:
1. 200 cigarettes or 50 cigars or 250 grams of tobacco
2. 1 liter of alcoholic drinks
3. 1.125 liters of perfume
4. Other products up to a value of CI$500

You are not permitted to bring in the following items:

Illegal drugs
Weapons
Ammunition
Endangered species
Counterfeit goods

Visa Categories and Eligibility

Here are the visa kinds and qualifications for the Cayman Islands.

Tourist Visa
1. Citizens of most countries may get a tourist visa for the Cayman Islands upon arrival.
2. The tourist visa is valid for 30 days and may be renewed for an additional 30 days.
3. To apply for a tourist visa, you will need to supply your passport, a current passport-style picture, and a completed visa application form.

Business Visa
1. Citizens of various nations, including China, India, and Russia, may need to get a business visa to visit the Cayman Islands.
2. The business visa is valid for 90 days and may be renewed for an additional 90 days.
3. To apply for a business visa, you will need to send your passport, a current passport-style picture, a completed visa application form, and a letter from your employer indicating the purpose of your visit.

Residential Visa
If you are expecting to remain in the Cayman Islands for longer than 90 days, you will need to secure a resident visa.
There are numerous sorts of resident visas available, including work visas, student visas, and investment visas.

To apply for a resident visa, you will need to supply your passport, a current passport-style picture, a completed visa application form, and supporting paperwork, such as a job offer letter, a letter of acceptance from a school, or proof of investment in the Cayman Islands.

Other Visas
There are a variety of different visas available for the Cayman Islands, including transit visas, medical visas, and diplomatic visas.

To apply for any of these visas, you will need to contact the Cayman Islands Immigration Department for additional information.

Visa Application Process
To apply for a visa for the Cayman Islands, you will need to complete these steps:

1. Visit the Cayman Islands Immigration Department webpage.
2. Click on the "Visas" tab.
3. Select the kind of visa you are seeking for.
4. Complete the online visa application form.
5. Pay the visa application cost.
6. Submit your application.

Visa Application Website
The website for the Cayman Islands Immigration Department is

https://www.gov.ky/immigration.

On this website, you can find information about visa requirements, application procedures, and fees. You can also apply for a visa online.

Visa Application Fee

The visa application cost for the Cayman Islands varies based on the kind of visa you are seeking for.

However, the regular charge is CI$100.

Visa Application Processing Time

The visa application processing period for the Cayman Islands varies based on the kind of visa you are seeking for. However, the usual processing period is 10-15 working days.

Visa Application Results

You will be advised of the outcomes of your visa application via email. If your visa application is granted, you will be given a visa sticker that you will need to display when you arrive in the Cayman Islands.

Travel Insurance

Travel insurance is a sort of insurance that protects you from unforeseen events that may happen while you are traveling, such as medical expenditures, trip cancellations, and lost baggage. It is necessary to get travel insurance before you go to the Cayman Islands.

Here are some of the perks of travel insurance:

Medical expenditures: Travel insurance will reimburse you for medical bills if you get sick or injured while you are traveling. This covers the expense of doctor's appointments, hospital stays, and prescription prescriptions.

Trip cancellation: Travel insurance will cover you if you have to cancel your trip due to a covered cause, such as a medical emergency, a natural catastrophe, or travel advice.

Lost baggage: Travel insurance can cover you if your luggage is lost or stolen while you are traveling.

This covers the expense of replacing your possessions. Several different travel insurance firms sell plans for the Cayman Islands. When picking a travel insurance policy, it is crucial to examine various plans and choose one that offers the coverage that you need. Here are a handful of the most popular travel insurance companies:

WORLD NOMADS
SAFETYWING
INSURED NOMADS
TRUE TRAVELER
AXA TRAVEL

When evaluating various travel insurance plans, it is vital to consider the following factors:

Coverage: Make sure that the insurance covers the risks that you are worried about, such as medical expenditures, trip cancellation, and lost baggage.

Cost: Travel insurance may be costly, so it is crucial to pick coverage that is reasonable for you.

Customer service: If you do have to make a claim, you will want to be sure that the travel insurance provider provides decent customer service.

Flight Options and Estimated Cost
From the US
American Airlines: Nonstop flights from Miami to Grand Cayman start at $150 round-trip.
Delta Airlines: Nonstop flights from Atlanta to Grand Cayman start at $175 round-trip.
United Airlines: Nonstop flights from Houston to Grand Cayman start at $200 round-trip.

JetBlue Airways: Nonstop flights from Boston to Grand Cayman start at $225 round-trip.

From the UK
British Airways: Nonstop flights from London Heathrow to Grand Cayman start at £374 round-trip.
Virgin Atlantic: Nonstop flights from London Gatwick to Grand Cayman start at £400 round-trip.
American Airlines: Nonstop flights from Miami to Grand Cayman start at £425 round-trip.
Delta Airlines: Nonstop flights from Atlanta to Grand Cayman start at £450 round-trip.

From Canada
Air Canada: Nonstop flights from Toronto to Grand Cayman start at $201 round-trip.
West Jet: Nonstop flights from Calgary to Grand Cayman start at $225 round-trip.
American Airlines: Nonstop flights from Miami to Grand Cayman start at $250 round-trip.
Delta Airlines: Nonstop flights from Atlanta to Grand Cayman start at $275 round-trip.

These are only a few examples, and many additional airlines operate flights to the Cayman Islands. When purchasing your travel, be careful to research rates and flight timings from several airlines to obtain the best bargain.

Here are some things to bear in mind when booking your ticket to the Cayman Islands:

1. The Cayman Islands are a popular tourist destination, therefore airfares might be pricey during high season.

2. If you are flexible with your trip dates, you may be able to get affordable flights.

3. Consider flying into a smaller airport, such as Owen Roberts International Airport on Grand Cayman, instead of the bigger George Town International Airport. Flights to smaller airports are frequently cheaper.

Money & Currency Exchange
The Cayman Islands Dollar is the official currency of the Cayman Islands. It is a pegged currency, which means that it is linked to the US Dollar at a rate of 0.83 KYD to 1 USD. This implies that the value of the Cayman Islands Dollar is always equal to 83% of the value of the US Dollar.

KYD stands for the Cayman Islands dollar, which is the national currency of the Cayman Islands.
KYD is the currency code used to denote the Cayman Islands dollar in financial transactions and currency exchange markets. The sign for the Cayman Islands dollar is "$" or "CI$", and it is usually referred to as CI$.

Let's take a look at the current exchange rates for the Cayman Islands Dollar (KYD) vs the US Dollar (USD), Euro (EUR), British Pound (GBP), and Canadian Dollar (CAD) as of March 2023:

Currency | Exchange Rate:

USD | 1 USD = 0.83 KYD
EUR | 1 EUR = 0.92 KYD
GBP | 1 GBP = 1.02 KYD
CAD | 1 CAD = 0.76 KYD

Please note that these currency rates are subject to change. The easiest approach to acquire the most up-to-date exchange rates is to utilize a currency converter.

If you are going to travel to the Cayman Islands, it is a good idea to convert some of your cash into Cayman Islands Dollars before you leave. Here are some of the top venues to convert currencies in the Cayman Islands:

Banks: Banks normally give the best conversion rates. However, they may offer restricted hours and may not be placed in convenient areas.

Currency exchange bureaus: Currency exchange bureaus are normally open longer hours than banks and are more widely placed. However, their exchange rates may not be as excellent as banks.

Hotels: Some hotels may exchange cash for their guests. However, their exchange rates are frequently not as excellent as banks or currency exchange agencies.

Here are some recommendations for converting cash in the Cayman Islands:

Do your research: Compare currency rates before you make a choice.

Be wary of costs: Some banks and currency exchange bureaus impose fees for exchanging currencies.

Consider using a credit card: Credit cards generally give better conversion rates than cash.

Be aware of scams: There have been instances of fraud involving money exchange in the Cayman Islands. Be careful to deal with reliable firms.

If you have any leftover Cayman Islands Dollars when you depart, you may convert them back into your native currency at a bank or currency exchange bureau.

Communication and Internet Access

1. Cellular service: The Cayman Islands offers great cellular service, with coverage across the islands. The two biggest suppliers are Digicel and FLOW. Both companies provide a range of options, including prepaid and postpaid contracts.

2. Internet access: The Cayman Islands also has strong internet service. There are a lot of providers, including Cable & Wireless, FLOW, and Digicel. All providers provide a range of services, including wired and cellular plans.

3. Wi-Fi: Wi-Fi is commonly accessible throughout the Cayman Islands, including at hotels, resorts, restaurants, cafés, and pubs. You may also find Wi-Fi at various public venues, such as libraries and parks.

4. Calling cards: Calling cards might be a useful choice for making international calls. You may get calling cards at most hotels, resorts, and convenience shops.

5. Public phones: Public phones are still accessible in the Cayman Islands, however, they are becoming more uncommon. If you need to use a public phone, you may find them in various post offices, libraries, and petrol stations.

Here are some ways for keeping connected while in the Cayman Islands:

1. Purchase a local SIM card: If you intend on using your mobile phone for calls, messages, and data, it is a good idea to purchase a local SIM card. You can acquire SIM cards at most mobile phone outlets.

2. Be wary of roaming charges: If you are using your phone from outside of your native country, you may be charged roaming costs. These costs may be costly, so it is vital to be aware of them before you use your phone.

Travel Cost and Budget

The Cayman Islands is a lovely and popular tourist destination, but it can also be an expensive one. Here is a summary of some of the expenditures you might anticipate paying on a vacation to the Cayman Islands:

Flights: Flights to the Cayman Islands may be pricey, particularly during the high season (December-April). From the US, expect to spend roughly $300-500 round-trip for a flight from a big city. From the UK, plan to spend roughly £400-600 round-trip.

Accommodation: Accommodation in the Cayman Islands may also be pricey. A budget-friendly alternative is to stay in a hostel, which may cost roughly $50-75 per night. A mid-range alternative is to stay in a hotel, which may cost roughly $100-200 per night. A premium alternative is to stay in a resort, which might cost roughly $200-300 per night or more.

Food: Food in the Cayman Islands may be pricey, particularly if you eat at restaurants. A budget-friendly alternative is to make your meals, which may cost roughly $20-30 per day. A mid-range alternative is to dine at informal eateries, which may cost roughly $30-50 per day. A luxury alternative is to dine at fine dining establishments, which may cost roughly $50-100 per day or more.

Activities: There are numerous things to do in the Cayman Islands, and many of them come with a price tag. Some popular activities include:

1. Snorkeling and diving: Snorkeling and diving are popular activities in the Cayman Islands, and there are many fantastic sites to explore. Snorkeling gear may be leased for roughly $20 per day, while diving gear can be rented for around $50 per day.

2. Sailing: Sailing is another popular sport in the Cayman Islands, and several firms provide sailing vacations. Sailing vacations might cost roughly $100-200 per person per day.

3. Fishing: Fishing is a popular sport in the Cayman Islands, and several charter companies provide fishing excursions. Fishing expeditions might cost roughly $100-200 per person per day.

4. Golf: Golf is another popular sport in the Cayman Islands, and there are numerous golf courses on the islands. Green fees may vary from $50-100 each round.

Transportation: Transportation in the Cayman Islands may be costly. Taxis are the most prevalent means of transportation, and rates may be exorbitant. A cab trip from the airport to George Town may cost roughly $20. You may also hire a vehicle, although this can also be pricey. Car rental fees might vary from $50-100 per day.

Here are some affordable possibilities for a vacation to the Cayman Islands for a solitary traveler, couple, and family of four
.

Estimated Budget for Solo Traveler
Accommodation: Hostel: $50-75 per night
Food: Cooking your meals: $20-30 per day
Activities: Snorkeling and diving: $20 per day
Transportation: Taxis: $20-30 per day
Other expenses: $100 per day
Total: $190-250 per day

Affordable Choices for Couple
Accommodation: Hotel: $100-200 per night
Food: Eating out at informal restaurants: $30-50 per day
Activities: Snorkeling and diving: $20 per day

Transportation: Taxis: $20-30 per day
Other expenses: $100 per day
Total: $300-400 per day

Budget Choices for a Family of Four
Accommodation: Resort: $200-300 per night
Food: Eating out at informal restaurants: $50-80 per day
Activities: Snorkeling and diving: $20 per day
Transportation: Taxis: $30-40 per day
Other expenses: $150 per day
Total: $500-650 per day

These are just some sample budgets, and you may be able to save money or spend more depending on your travel style. For example, if you are prepared to stay in a less costly hotel or hostel, you may save money on lodging. If you are willing to make your meals, you may save money on food. And if you are ready to explore the island on foot or by bicycle, you may save money on transportation.

No matter what your budget is, a vacation to the Cayman Islands may be a very pleasurable and memorable experience.

MUSEUMS AND ART GALLERIES

CAYMAN
ISLAND

Step into the lively realm of Caymanian culture and creative expression. In this Chapter, it's time to discover the rich past and creative energy of the Cayman Islands via its museums and art galleries. Immerse yourself in interesting exhibitions, explore local artwork, and obtain a greater grasp of the islands' history and creative traditions.

1. National Gallery of the Cayman Islands:

The National Gallery of the Cayman Islands (NGCI) was created in 1996 by Caymanian artists and art aficionados. Its purpose is to conserve and promote Caymanian art while developing an appreciation for art and culture in the Cayman Islands.

With approximately 1,000 artworks ranging from paintings to sculptures, prints, and photos, the NGCI collection extends from the 19th century to the modern day, showcasing Caymanian creative expressions. The gallery features changing exhibits showcasing local and worldwide artists, complimented by engaging educational activities including art courses, seminars, and talks.
Special activities like concerts, film screenings, and literary readings further enhance the NGCI experience.

Location: The National Gallery of the Cayman Islands is situated in George Town, the capital city of the Cayman Islands. Its address is Esterley Tibbetts Highway, George Town, Grand Cayman.

Opening and Closing Hours: The gallery is open from Monday through Saturday, from 10:00 AM to 5:00 PM. It is closed on Sundays and public holidays.

Accessibility & Wheelchair Access: The National Gallery of the Cayman Islands is dedicated to providing access to all visitors. The facility is handicapped accessible, with ramps and elevators provided for easier accessibility.

Admission cost and Tickets: As of now, there is an admission cost for visiting the National Gallery. The charge is CI$10 for adults. There is a 10% discount for students and elderly with ID. Children under 12 years old enter for free. Please note that rates are subject to change, so it's important to check the official website for the most up-to-date pricing information.

Online Ticketing Choices: The National Gallery of the Cayman Islands provides online ticketing choices for increased convenience. Visitors may buy their tickets in advance on the official website, allowing for smooth access upon arrival.

Visitor Rules and Etiquette: To provide a good experience for all visitors, the National Gallery of the Cayman Islands has a few standards in place. Guests are requested to appreciate the artwork and create a peaceful and courteous attitude throughout the galleries. Photography is permitted but without flash or tripod, to preserve the artwork.
It's also encouraged to keep from handling the exhibits unless specified differently. Food and drink are not allowed within the gallery.

Weather and Comfort: The gallery is an inside facility, offering a pleasant setting regardless of the weather conditions outside. It's a terrific alternative for a cultural experience, particularly on hot or wet days when outdoor activities may be less pleasant.

Personal Review: I found the National Gallery of the Cayman Islands to be a lovely and educational museum. The collection comprises a broad range of artwork, from traditional Caymanian paintings and sculptures to modern and contemporary items. I admired the show of pieces by Caymanian artist Al Ebanks. The gallery also provides a range of educational programs and activities, making it a perfect venue to learn about Caymanian art and culture.

2. Cayman Islands National Museum:

The Cayman Islands National Museum, situated in the Old Courts Building from the 1830s, boasts a rich history. Originally a courthouse and prison, it has also been a post office, library, and savings bank. In 1986, it became the Cayman Islands National Museum.

With nearly 8,000 objects, the museum highlights the Cayman Islands' unique past. From Arawak and Taino heritage through the British colonial period and early tourism, the collection covers the islands' history. The museum's goal is to conserve and showcase Caymanian history.

It does this via permanent and temporary displays of history and culture, educational programs for all ages, and exciting public events like concerts and festivals.

Location: The Cayman Islands National Museum is situated at 64 Seafarers Way, George Town, Grand Cayman.

Opening and Closing Hours: The museum is open Monday to Friday from 9:00 AM to 5:00 PM and on Saturdays from 10:00 AM to 2:00 PM. It is closed on Sundays and public holidays.

Accessibility & Wheelchair Access: The museum is wheelchair accessible, ensuring that visitors with mobility problems may easily browse the exhibits. Ramps and elevators are provided for convenient access to various floors of the museum.

Admission charge and Tickets: Currently, the admission charge for adults is KYD 8, while children aged 6-12 may enter for KYD 4. Children under 6 years old may enter for free. There is a family rate of $20 for two adults and two children.

Online Ticketing: The museum provides online ticketing alternatives, enabling visitors to buy their tickets in advance and escape the ticketing lineups upon arrival. This useful solution helps save time and assures seamless admission into the museum.

Visitor Rules and Etiquette: Visitors are requested to respect the exhibits and maintain a peaceful and tidy atmosphere. Photography is permitted in most sections of the museum, but it's vital to be cautious of any special limits or rules that may be in place for individual exhibitions.

Weather and Comfort: The museum is an indoor institution, offering a pleasant and climate-controlled setting for visitors. This makes it a wonderful alternative for exploring and learning about the history and culture of the Cayman Islands, regardless of the weather outside. Visitors are recommended to wear comfortable clothes and sunscreen. The museum features a variety of indoor exhibitions, so it is also a good idea to carry a hat and sunglasses.

Personal Review: I enjoyed my visit to the Cayman Islands National Museum. I thought the displays to be educational and well-curated. It gave me the chance to learn more about the history and culture of the Cayman Islands.

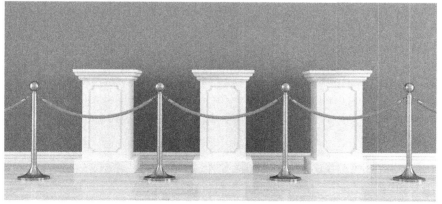

3. Guy Harvey Gallery and Shoppe:

The Guy Harvey Gallery and Shoppe, created in 1993 by famous marine artist, scientist, and environmentalist Guy Harvey, is a popular tourist site in Grand Cayman. It shows a broad array of Guy Harvey artwork, including paintings, prints, sculptures, and garments.

The gallery is not just a center for artwork and souvenirs but also actively supports marine conservation, cooperating with numerous groups to raise awareness about saving the ocean and its people.

Location: The Guy Harvey Gallery and Shoppe are situated in George Town, Grand Cayman, within proximity to the shoreline and the lively commercial sector. Its actual location is 45 South Church Street, George Town, Grand Cayman.

Opening and Closing Hours: The gallery is open Monday to Saturday from 9:00 AM to 5:00 PM. It is closed on Sundays.
Accessibility & Wheelchair Access: The gallery is accessible to persons with mobility impairments since it includes wheelchair access and ramps for simple travel. Visitors may visit the exhibitions comfortably, regardless of their mobility.

Admission charge and Tickets: There is no admission charge or ticket necessary to access the Guy Harvey Gallery and Shoppe. Visitors may freely wander the gallery and peruse the numerous marine-themed artworks and products on show.

Discount Rates: While precise specifics concerning discounts for students and seniors may differ, it's wise to enquire at the gallery about any available discounts or promotions that may be relevant.

Online Ticketing: The gallery does not normally need online ticketing, since it does not have an entry price.

Visitors may just go in and enjoy the exhibits and merchandise.

Visitor Rules and Etiquette: Visitors are asked to respect the artwork and exhibitions, refraining from touching or messing with the objects. Photography is normally permitted, however, it's encouraged to check with the gallery personnel for any special limitations or rules that may be in place.

Weather and Comfort: The gallery is an indoor institution, offering a pleasant and air-conditioned atmosphere for visitors. This enables a pleasurable experience regardless of the weather conditions outside.

Personal Review: Here are some of the things that I loved about the Guy Harvey Gallery and Shoppe:
1. The artwork is stunning and motivating.
2. The gallery is an excellent location to learn about marine conservation.
3. The staff is nice and competent.
4. The gallery is an excellent spot to purchase souvenirs and presents.

Here are some of the things that should be improved:
1. The gallery could be a little more kid-friendly.
2. The pricing may be a little cheaper.
3. The gallery might be a little more centrally positioned.

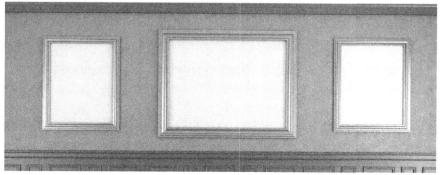

4. The Ritz-Carlton Art Gallery:

The Ritz-Carlton Art Gallery, created in 1983 by Horst Schulze, the originator of The Ritz-Carlton Hotel Company, highlights local and regional artists while fostering cultural interchange. With over 10,000 artists and 100 shows, it has become a worldwide known gallery, acknowledged with the coveted Pegasus Award for Excellence in the Arts.

The gallery reflects a passion for art and allows people an opportunity to admire its beauty and learn about other civilizations. It provides a platform for artists to present their work and engage with a worldwide audience, reflecting the perfect balance of art, culture, and hospitality inside The Ritz-Carlton Hotel Company.

Location: The Ritz-Carlton Art Gallery is housed inside The Ritz-Carlton resort, located at Seven Mile Beach, Grand Cayman. The actual location is West Bay Road, Seven Mile Beach, KY1-1209, Cayman Islands.

Opening and Closing Hours: The gallery's opening hours may change, therefore it's advised to check the current schedule. Generally, the gallery is open from 9 am to 5 pm, every day.

Accessible & Wheelchair Access: The Ritz-Carlton resort is noted for its accessible facilities, including wheelchair ramps, elevators, and large hallways, guaranteeing that guests with mobility issues may move about easily throughout the art museum.

Admission charge and Tickets: There is no admission charge for the gallery.

Visitor Rules and Etiquette: As with any art museum, visitors are required to obey certain rules and etiquette.

These may include abstaining from touching the artwork, keeping a peaceful and courteous setting, and obeying any rules offered by gallery officials. Visitors are encouraged to dress properly and to avoid carrying food or beverages into the gallery. Photography is allowed in the gallery however, flash photography is not authorized.

Weather & Comfort: The Ritz-Carlton Art Gallery is an inside facility, offering a pleasant setting regardless of the weather outside. Visitors may appreciate the artworks and exhibitions in a climate-controlled atmosphere, offering a comfortable experience.

Personal Review: I thought the displays to be educational and well-curated. I loved the chance to learn more about the art and culture of the Cayman Islands.

Historical Sites and Landmarks

1. Fort George:

Fort George, situated in George Town, Grand Cayman, is a historic fort established in 1790 to safeguard the island from foreign invaders.

It replaced a previous fort destroyed by a storm in 1788. Used as a military post until 1901, it thereafter fulfilled numerous roles. Donated to the National Trust in 1990, the renovated fort has been available to the public since 1994.

Today, it's a famous tourist site giving historical insights, and scenic views of the port and city, and acts as a setting for weddings and gatherings. Fort George serves as a tribute to the Cayman Islands' tenacity, history, and the value of peace and security.

Location: Fort George is located on the southeastern shore of Grand Cayman, overlooking the George Town Harbor. Its address is 63 Fort Street, George Town, Grand Cayman.

Opening and Closing Hours: The fort is open to tourists Monday to Friday from 8:30 AM to 4:30 PM. It is closed on weekends and public holidays.

Accessibility & Wheelchair Access: The fort is not wheelchair accessible, since it is positioned on a slope with rough ground and steps. Visitors with mobility issues may find it challenging to explore the fort's structures.

Admission Charge: There is an admission fee of $10 for adults, $5 for children ages 5-12, and free for children under 5.

Discounts: There is a discount for students and elders. Students with valid IDs may get in for $5, while seniors (65+) can get in for $7.50.

Online tickets: There is no online ticketing option for Fort George. Tickets must be bought at the fort.

Visitor Rules and Etiquette: Visitors are urged to be courteous of the fort and its grounds. No smoking, drinking, or trash is permitted. Visitors are also requested to remain on the trails and not climb on the walls. Additionally, trash is strictly forbidden, and visitors are asked to keep the area clean and neat.

Weather and Comfort: Fort George is an outdoor destination, thus it is essential to check the weather forecast before going. Wear comfortable footwear and consider carrying sun protection, such as a hat, sunscreen, and drink to remain hydrated.

Photography: Photography is permitted at Fort George, and tourists are invited to capture the spectacular vistas of George Town and the harbor. However, it's crucial to be respectful of other guests and avoid impeding routes or interrupting the experience of others. Also, flash photography is not permitted within the fort.

Personal Review: I loved seeing Fort George. It is a little fort, but it is well-maintained and has a lot of history, and you can probably see everything in about 30 minutes. The views from the fort are equally stunning. I would suggest visiting Fort George if you are interested in Caymanian history or if you are seeking a site to shoot some photographs.

There are a few displays and cannons to see, and you can also wander about the fort and enjoy the views. If you want to take your time and read all of the exhibits, you may need a little extra time. But if you're on a tight schedule, 30 minutes should be plenty to view the fort.

2. Mission home:

The Mission House in Bodden Town, Grand Cayman, is a historic home that earned popularity in the 1800s. It gained the name "Mission House" owing to the presence of early missionaries, teachers, and families who founded a Presbyterian church and school in Bodden Town.

Originally erected in the 1700s, the home was bought by the Presbyterian Church in 1832. Missionaries played a major role in teaching Christianity and Western education to the Caymanian people, running one of the earliest schools on the island.

After falling into disrepair, the National Trust for the Cayman Islands seized control of the Mission House in 1999, restoring it to its former glory. Now a famous tourist destination, the Mission House also holds other events. It serves as a reminder of the Cayman Islands' early Christian and educational origins, as well as the value of community and teamwork.

Location: Mission House is located at 63 Gun Square Road, Bodden Town, Grand Cayman.

Opening and Closing Hours: The home is open for visitors from Monday through Friday, between 9:30 AM and 5:30 PM. It is closed on weekends and public holidays.

Accessible & Wheelchair Access: Mission House has wheelchair accessible, so that guests with mobility problems may tour the property pleasantly. Ramps and accessible paths are offered for easier navigation.

Admission Charge: There is an admission fee of $10 for adults, $5 for children ages 5-12, and free for children under 5.
Discounts: There is a discount for students and elders. Students with valid IDs may get in for $5, while seniors (65+) can get in for $7.50.

Online Tickets: There is no online ticketing option for the Mission House. Tickets must be bought at the house.

Visitors Norms & Etiquettes: Visitors are urged to be respectful of the home and its grounds. No smoking, drinking, or trash is permitted. Visitors are also urged to keep on the walks and not climb on the furniture.

Weather and Comfort: Mission House is mostly an outdoor location, thus it's important to check the weather conditions before your visit. Dress comfortably, use sunscreen, and carry a hat or umbrella to cover yourself from the sun. There are shaded places provided on-site for tourists' comfort.

Photography: Photography is permitted at the Mission House. However, flash photography is not permitted inside the residence.

Personal Review: It is a little house, but it is well-maintained and has a lot of history. The house is also quite picturesque. I would suggest visiting the Mission House if you are interested in Caymanian history or if you are seeking for a site to shoot some photographs.

3. Queen Elizabeth II Botanic Park:

The Queen Elizabeth II Botanic Park is a non-profit garden and wildlife facility in Grand Cayman. Owned jointly by the Cayman Islands Government and the National Trust for the Cayman Islands, it works to protect natural areas and historic landmarks.

Established in 1994, it contains attractions including the Visitor Centre, Floral Garden, Orchid Boardwalk, Xerophytic Garden, Heritage Garden, Woodland Trail, and the forthcoming Children's Garden.

Home to numerous flora and animals, including the endangered Grand Cayman Blue Iguana, the park provides educational programs and activities. It acts as a center for natural enjoyment, environmental education, and conservation activism, benefitting both residents and visitors alike.

Location: Queen Elizabeth II Botanic Park is located on Frank Sound Road, North Side, Grand Cayman, Cayman Islands.
Opening and Closing Hours: The park is open to visitors from Monday through Sunday, from 9:00 AM to 5:30 PM. It is accessible throughout the year, enabling you to enjoy its beauty at your leisure.

Accessible & Wheelchair Access: The park provides accessibility for wheelchair users and those with reduced mobility. Ramps and concrete paths enable seamless access to different regions of the park.

Admission Charge: The admission fee is $15 for adults, $10 for children ages 5-12, and free for children under 5.
Discounts: There is a discount for students and elders. Students with valid IDs may get in for $10, while seniors (65+) can get in for $12.50.

Online Tickets: There is an online ticketing option for the Queen Elizabeth II Botanic Park. Tickets may be bought here: https://www.botanic-park.ky/

Visitor Rules and Etiquette: To conserve the natural beauty of the park, visitors are politely encouraged to follow the designated walkways, abstain from plucking or destroying flora, and appreciate the tranquility of the surroundings. It is also essential to bring bug repellent and sun protection, as well as to remain on authorized routes for safety considerations.

Weather and Comfort: The park provides a nice outdoor experience, with covered places and mild breezes. However, it's essential to check the weather forecast and dress properly, particularly during warmer months. Comfortable walking shoes, sunscreen, and hats are advised.

Photography: Photography is permitted in the Queen Elizabeth II Botanic Park. However, flash photography is not permitted within the greenhouses.

Personal review: It is a lovely park with a variety of plants and flowers. I appreciated the Orchid Trail and the lake. I would suggest visiting the park if you are interested in plants and flowers or if you are searching for a pleasant area to unwind.

4. Mastic Trail:

The Mastic Trail is a 2.3-mile (3.7 km) hiking trail situated in the Mastic Reserve on Grand Cayman Island. It runs through varied environments including mangrove swamps and woods, exhibiting the mastic tree. Originally established by Caymanians in the 1800s, the path eased movement between communities. Restored in the 1970s, it has become a famous tourist site for trekking, birding, and enjoying the island's natural heritage.

The route is recognized for its importance in the conservation and protection of natural resources. It depicts Caymanian innovation, perseverance, and the island's exceptional beauty and variety. Beyond its recreational appeal, the route acts as a gorgeous setting for weddings and photo shoots, adding its attraction.

Location: The Mastic Trail is situated in the center section of Grand Cayman, winding through the Mastic Reserve. It may be accessible via Frank Sound Road in North Side or South Side Road in Bodden Town.

Opening and Closing Hours: The path is open every day from 8:00 AM to 4:30 PM. It's suggested to start your trip early to enable adequate time to explore and appreciate the trail's splendor.

Accessibility & Wheelchair Access: The Mastic route is a natural route with rocky terrain, making it tough for wheelchair access. The track is particularly suitable for hikers with intermediate fitness levels and solid boots.

Admission Charge and Tickets: There is no admission charge for the path. However, there is a recommended gift of $5 per participant.

Visitor Rules and Etiquette: Stay on the path. Do not disrupt the vegetation or animals.

Be considerate to other hikers. Leave no trace.

Weather & Comfort: The path may be hot and humid, so it's suggested to wear lightweight and breathable clothes, comfortable walking shoes, and pack adequate water and sun protection. Mosquito repellant may also be important, particularly at certain periods of the year.

Photography: Photography is permitted and encouraged along the Mastic Trail. Capture the beauty of the flora and wildlife, but remember to be polite and not damage the natural environment when shooting images.

Personal Review: It was a terrific opportunity to view some of the natural beauty of Grand Cayman. I observed a variety of flora and creatures, and I even got to witness a Caymanian blue iguana. The trek was a little tough, but it was worth it for the views. Here is some extra advice for trekking the Mastic Trail:
Go early in the morning to escape the heat.

Bring a map and compass.
Let someone know where you are going.
Be prepared for everything, even rain.

5. Wreck of the Ten Sail:

The Wreck of the Ten Sail, an 18th-century shipwreck off the East End of Grand Cayman, is a historic occurrence.

Despite the loss of eight lives, locals valiantly rescued the crew and passengers of 10 destroyed ships from the convoy.

Today, a park acts as a monument to memorialize the night of the tragedy. The Maritime Trail brings tourists to the reef where the ships met their end, while a cliff shows dangerous Ironshore and a monument to the fallen. In 1994, Queen Elizabeth II and Prince Philip dedicated the park on the 200th anniversary of the incident. The Wreck of the Ten Sail serves as a reminder of the hazards of the sea, the power of community, and the courage demonstrated by the Caymanian people.

Location: The Wreck of the Ten Sail is situated off the shore of East End, Grand Cayman. The precise position is noted by a monument on the cliffs of the East End Lighthouse Park.

Opening and Closing Hours: The facility is open to the public at all times, since it is an outdoor venue. Visitors may explore the monument and enjoy the spectacular views of the surrounding region anytime they wish to come.

Accessibility & Wheelchair Access: The accessibility of the site may vary since it is placed on natural terrain. While there may be some roads and designated viewing spots, it's vital to remember that the site's harsh environment could cause difficulty for persons with mobility impairments.

Admission Fee and Tickets: The Wreck of the Ten Sail is a public monument, therefore there is no admission fee or ticket necessary to visit. It is freely open to all visitors.

Visitor Rules & Etiquette: Visitors are urged to be courteous of the park and its grounds.

No smoking, drinking, or trash is permitted. Visitors are also requested to remain on the trails and not climb on the rocks.

Weather and Comfort: As the Wreck of the Ten Sail is an outdoor sight, visitors should consider the weather conditions. It is essential to dress properly for the environment and wear comfortable footwear for walking on difficult terrain.

Photography: Photography is normally permitted at the location, and visitors are free to document their experience. However, it's crucial to be careful and respectful of others' privacy and any written prohibitions on photographing.

Personal Review: The Wreck of the Ten Sail is an interesting spot to see. It is a reminder of a horrible incident in Caymanian history, but it is also a monument to the tenacity of the Caymanian people. I would suggest visiting the Wreck of the Ten Sail if you are interested in Caymanian history or if you are searching for a site to shoot some photographs.

6. Hell Post Office:

Hell Post Office, located in the village of Hell on Grand Cayman's West Bay Road, is a must-visit tourist destination. Named for its unusual beachfront of jagged black limestone and lava rock, this post office has been operational since 1964.

The lovely wooden structure includes a red roof and proudly displays a sign identifying it as the only post office globally with a permanent stamp cancellation saying "HELL." Here, visitors may mail postcards and letters emblazoned with the distinctive "Hell" postmark.

Additionally, the post office includes a lovely gift store where travelers may buy souvenirs and items branded with the word "Hell." A visit to Hell Post Office offers a thrilling and amusing experience, great for sharing a laugh or sending a unique postcard from this unusual site.

Location: Hell Post Office is located in the West Bay district of Grand Cayman, near the famed tourist attraction of Hell. Its actual location is 228 Hell Road, West Bay, Grand Cayman.

Opening and Closing Hours: The post office runs from Monday to Friday, opening at 9:00 AM and closing at 5:00 PM. It is closed on weekends and public holidays.

Accessibility & Wheelchair Access: The post office is fully accessible to guests of all abilities. It enables wheelchair access, enabling a pleasant and inclusive experience for everyone.

Admission Charge and Tickets: There is no admission charge or ticket necessary to enter Hell Post Office. It is a free attraction that allows people to explore and take part in its unique postal offers.

Visitor Rules and Etiquette: Visitors are urged to be courteous of the grounds and follow any recommendations offered by the personnel. As it is a functional post office, visitors should be cautious of anyone utilizing the facilities for postal reasons and keep a polite manner.

Weather and Comfort: Hell Post Office is an outdoor attraction, thus the comfort level may vary based on the weather conditions. It is essential to check the weather forecast and dress properly to ensure a pleasant stay.

Photography: Photography is permitted at Hell Post Office, allowing a chance to capture unique moments and the peculiar ambiance of the site, although flash photography is not allowed within the post office. However, it's always polite to seek permission before snapping photographs of other guests or staff members.

Personal review: It is a little post office, but it is well-maintained and has a lot of charm.
The sign outside the post office is a lot of fun, and it is a fantastic site to send a postcard from Hell.

Cultural Festivals and Events

The Cayman Islands is a dynamic destination that celebrates its rich cultural history via different festivals and events. Here are some of the noteworthy cultural festivals and events in the Cayman Islands.

Annual Festivals and Celebrations

1. Pirates Week Festival: Pirates Week Festival is a colorful and exciting festival that takes place in November each year. It reflects the islands' pirate heritage and pays honor to the maritime past. As I went through the colorful streets of George Town, the atmosphere was electrifying with the sounds of live music, the laughter of residents and tourists, and the remarkable sight of individuals dressed in pirate costumes.

The celebration covers several days, involving a spectacular procession packed with artistically made floats and energetic participants. I couldn't help but participate in the infectious enthusiasm as the audience roared at the daring pirates. Street dances took place during the celebrations, when everyone was welcome to dance to catchy Caribbean beats.

Fireworks lit the night sky, giving a touch of enchantment to the celebrations. From treasure hunts to historical reenactments, there was an abundance of activities for all ages. Food vendors dotted the streets, providing wonderful local food and cool drinks.

2. Batabano Carnival: Batabano Carnival is a dynamic and colorful event that unfolds in May, encapsulating the spirit of Caribbean culture. The carnival signifies solidarity, self-expression, and fun. If you join the parade procession, you'll be amazed by the stunning costumes covered with feathers, sequins, and brilliant colors.

The throbbing sounds of soca and calypso music filled the air as revelers danced around the streets. The excitement is intoxicating, and you wouldn't be able to avoid dancing to the beat. People of different backgrounds gathered together, enjoying the spirit of freedom and festivity.

The centerpiece of the carnival is the bright float displays, each one reflecting a different subject or part of Caymanian culture. The inventiveness and attention to detail is simply awe-inspiring. Food sellers featured a range of Caribbean cuisines, while local craftsmen showed their crafts.

3. Cayman Cookout: Cayman Cookout is a gastronomic spectacular that takes place in January, highlighting the islands' gourmet food sector and drawing famous chefs from across the globe. The festival represents culinary quality, innovation, and the appreciation of tastes. The scent of wonderful meals floods the air, enticing one's taste senses.

The event offered culinary demos, interactive seminars, and unique dining experiences. I once got the unique chance to witness top chefs in action, learning their skills and secrets. Tastings enabled me to taste the culinary masterpieces, which mixed local ingredients with foreign influences.

Engaging in panel discussions and presentations emphasized the shifting culinary trends and the necessity of sustainable practices. The environment was humming with enthusiasm, and I found myself involved in chats with other food fans and industry experts.

Each event highlighted the islanders' zeal for life, their love for their traditions, and their welcoming welcome. Whether you're a culinary lover, a history buff, or just seeking a memorable experience, these yearly festivals in the Cayman Islands are not to be missed.

Music Festivals

1. KAABOO Cayman: KAABOO Cayman is an annual music and arts event that takes place on the stunning Seven Mile Beach in Grand Cayman. The festival epitomizes the perfect escape, featuring a combination of music, art, comedy, gourmet delights, and more. I had the privilege of visiting KAABOO Cayman last year, and it was a fantastic experience.

The event presents an incredible array of prominent performers, bands, and artists from diverse genres. From rock and pop to reggae and techno, there's something for everyone's musical taste. I was amazed by the dynamic acts and the stunning background of the Caribbean Sea.

Apart from the music, KAABOO Cayman also features stunning artwork and installations, making it a feast for the eyes. The event grounds are tastefully adorned, providing a vivid and immersive environment.

The festival takes place over numerous days, generally in February. Attendees can anticipate a mix of well-known headliners and rising performers, offering a chance to discover new talents. In addition to the music, there are comedy acts, culinary demos, and interactive activities to enjoy.

2. Cayman Islands Jazz Festival: The Cayman Islands Jazz Festival is a passionate festival of jazz music hosted in George Town, the capital of the Cayman Islands. As a jazz aficionado, attending this event was a dream come true. The event represents the confluence of cultures and the power of music to unite people.

The performances are staged in numerous places, including outdoor stages and smaller spaces, creating a varied and immersive experience

I was mesmerized by the sweet melodies, improvisations, and deep sounds that filled the air.

The event normally takes place in December and comprises both local and international jazz musicians. From traditional jazz to current versions, the roster displays the variety of the genre. It's a fantastic time to relax, unwind, and allow the lovely rhythms to carry you to another planet.

3. Cayman Arts Festival: The Cayman Arts Festival is an annual event that honors the performing arts, including music, dance, and theater. This event takes place in several sites around the Cayman Islands, displaying the rich cultural history and creative abilities of the islands.

I had the privilege of visiting the Cayman Arts Festival in George Town, and it was a wonderfully immersive experience. The event highlights the ingenuity and enthusiasm of the local artists' community.

The events feature exciting concerts, recitals, and seminars by both local and international performers. From classical music to contemporary dance, there's a vast spectrum of cultural forms to appreciate. I was astonished by the level of ability and the passion of the performers.

The Cayman Arts Festival normally takes place over many weeks, featuring a comprehensive calendar of activities. It's a terrific chance to observe the beauty and power of the performing arts while supporting the local cultural community.

Whether you're a music aficionado, jazz lover, or a follower of the performing arts, these events in the Cayman Islands provide remarkable experiences. From the breathtaking surroundings to the wide array of performers, they bring the spirit of music and art to life, providing moments of pleasure, inspiration, and connection.

Sporting Events and Competitions

1. Cayman Islands Marathon: The Cayman Islands Marathon takes place on Grand Cayman, commencing and ending in George Town.

I had the honor of watching the Cayman Islands Marathon, and I can assure you that the enthusiasm and excitement were obvious as athletes from around the globe arrived to take on the hard route. The marathon signifies perseverance, dedication, and a celebration of the human spirit.

The marathon normally takes place in December, when the weather is suitable for running. Participants may anticipate a well-organized event with multiple racing categories, including a full marathon, half marathon, and relay choices. The route takes runners through the picturesque coastal roads, affording stunning views of the Caribbean Sea.

2. Cayman Islands International Fishing Tournament: The Cayman Islands International Fishing Tournament is normally held in the seas around Grand Cayman, bringing fishermen from near and far.

While I haven't personally attended the fishing event, I've heard fantastic accounts from aficionados who have participated. The competition represents the love for the sea, fraternity among fishermen, and the excitement of the pursuit.

This fascinating contest normally takes place in May, when the fishing conditions are optimum. Participants compete to capture numerous fish species, including marlin, tuna, wahoo, and mahi-mahi. Anglers should anticipate a pleasant but competitive environment, with prizes handed out for the greatest catches.

3. Cayman Islands Classic (Basketball competition): The Cayman Islands Classic basketball competition is hosted at the John Gray High School Gymnasium in George Town, Grand Cayman.

I haven't visited the Cayman Islands Classic, but it has earned a reputation for showcasing great college basketball teams from the United States and abroad. The event reflects the spirit of competitiveness, sportsmanship, and passion for the game.

This spectacular basketball competition generally takes place in November. Fans can expect high-intensity contests, as teams fight it out on the court. The event gives a chance to observe exceptional athletes in action and experience the exciting atmosphere of a live sports event.

4. Flowers Sea Swim: The Flowers Sea Swim takes place at Seven Mile Beach in Grand Cayman. Though I haven't been there for the Flowers Sea Swim, I've heard fantastic reports from swimmers who have participated. This swim signifies perseverance, appreciation for the water, and the enjoyment of Cayman's natural beauty.

The Flowers Sea Swim, generally held in June, is one of the world's greatest open-water swimming competitions. Participants of all ages and ability levels converge to swim along the gorgeous Seven Mile Beach. With numerous race durations available, including a one-mile swim, it's an inclusive event that emphasizes the pleasure of swimming in the crystal-clear Caribbean seas.

5. Legends Tennis Tournament: The Legends Tennis Tournament is held at The Ritz-Carlton, Grand Cayman. While I haven't visited the Legends Tennis Tournament firsthand, I've heard it described as a fantastic event that invites renowned tennis players to the island.
The event represents the passion for tennis, the celebration of athletic success, and the chance for spectators to watch tennis in action.

The Legends Tennis Tournament normally takes place in November, bringing past tennis greats who exhibit their abilities on the court. Tennis aficionados can look forward to thrilling matches, up-close contact with the players, and the opportunity to see the lasting brilliance of some of the sport's giants.

These athletic events and contests in the Cayman Islands provide fascinating experiences, exhibiting the islands' enthusiasm for sports, outdoor activities, and the celebration of human accomplishments. Whether you're a player or a spectator, these events give you a chance to immerse yourself in the lively athletic culture of the Cayman Islands and create amazing experiences.

Exploring
Grand
Cayman

Chapter 3

Introduction to Grand Cayman

Welcome to Grand Cayman, the biggest and most developed island in the gorgeous Cayman Islands. As a tourist who has been lucky enough to explore this wonderful island, let me provide a peek at the treasures that await you.

Picture yourself sunbathing in the sun on the legendary Seven Mile Beach, feeling the fine sand between your toes and the lovely ocean wind on your skin. Dive into the captivating underwater world, where bright coral reefs and friendly marine life make a veritable paradise for snorkelers and divers. Immerse yourself in the island's rich culture, enjoying the tastes of local food and feeling the warmth of Caymanian hospitality.

With an assortment of luxurious resorts, exhilarating water sports, and hidden treasures waiting to be found, Grand Cayman provides a compelling mix of fun and adventure.

George Town: The Capital City

George Town, the capital city of the Cayman Islands, possesses a rich history and provides a wealth of attractions that pull in people from across the globe. Established in the 18th century, George Town has grown from a modest village to a busy hub of trade, culture, and tourism.

This dynamic city is recognized for its strong financial industry, housing several offshore banks and financial organizations. It serves as a key worldwide financial center, drawing foreign enterprises and experts. The skyline is decorated with contemporary office buildings, emphasizing the city's economic strength.

George Town is a popular location for travelers, providing a range of activities to suit diverse interests.

The city features an assortment of duty-free stores, boutiques, and premium brands, making it a shopping heaven for travelers seeking retail therapy.

The waterfront area and Camana Bay are crowded with restaurants, bars, and entertainment opportunities, providing a dynamic scene.

The city is home to the Cayman Islands National Museum, where visitors may dig into the islands' rich past and see exhibits displaying the natural history, cultural customs, and maritime legacy. Fort George, a historic stronghold, gives an insight into the island's military history.

One of the city's most prominent sights is the Cayman Islands Legislative Assembly Building, a majestic colonial-style monument that serves as the seat of government. The nearby Heroes Square pays honor to the national heroes of the Cayman Islands.

While George Town has various virtues, it also confronts issues such as traffic congestion, particularly during cruise ship days when visitors throng to the area. However, the city's attempts to modernize infrastructure and transportation systems remain continuing.

With a population of around 30,000 persons, George Town is a busy town that caters to both locals and visitors. Its cosmopolitan character, cultural variety, and energetic environment make it a wonderful place to explore and enjoy the finest of the Cayman Islands.

Seven Mile Beach: Sun, Sand, and Fun

Seven Mile Beach, widely described as one of the most beautiful beaches in the Caribbean, is a tropical paradise that provides sun, sand, and unlimited fun. Stretching along the western coast of Grand Cayman, this gorgeous beach is a favorite destination for both residents and visitors alike.

With its crystal-clear turquoise seas, pure white beaches, and magnificent sunsets, Seven Mile Beach offers a gorgeous backdrop for leisure and enjoyment. The beach runs for around 6 miles, allowing adequate area for beachgoers to soak up the sun, swim in the placid seas, and indulge in different water sports activities.

Seven Mile Beach is noted for its world-class resorts, luxury residences, and beachfront hotels that cater to travelers wanting a lavish beach break. The beachfront villas provide spectacular views, direct access to the beach, and a choice of facilities to guarantee an enjoyable stay.

Aside from sunbathing and swimming, Seven Mile Beach provides a broad choice of leisure activities. Water sports lovers may delight in snorkeling, paddle-boarding, kayaking, and jet skiing, discovering the vivid marine life and undersea treasures. The quiet and clean waters make it a perfect site for novices and seasoned water enthusiasts alike.

The beach is dotted with a variety of beach bars, restaurants, and cafés where tourists may enjoy wonderful local food, tropical cocktails, and refreshing beverages. Whether it's a casual seaside café or a fancy dining establishment, Seven Mile Beach provides alternatives to suit every palate.

While Seven Mile Beach is a famous tourist attraction, it yet manages to keep its natural beauty and calm environment. The beach is scrupulously maintained, and efforts are taken to protect the natural environment. Visitors are asked to respect the beach's natural environment and conduct responsible tourism.

With its picturesque location, smooth beaches, and turquoise seas, Seven Mile Beach captivates tourists with its pure beauty and provides a tropical retreat like no other.

Whether you're seeking leisure, adventure, or just a spot to unwind and soak up the sun, Seven Mile Beach is a must-visit site that will leave you with treasured memories of a real caribbean paradise.

Extra Information on Seven Mile Beach:

Opening and Closing hours: As a public beach, Seven Mile Beach does not have fixed opening and closing hours. Visitors may access the beach at any time of the day, giving them flexibility in organizing their beach activities.

Accessibility: Accessibility to Seven Mile Beach is great, with multiple access points and parking places available along the shore. The beach is readily accessible by both private and public transportation.

Wheelchair access is available at certain spots throughout the beach, making it inclusive for guests with mobility issues. These access points often include ramps or paths leading to the beach area.

Admission Charge: There is no admission charge or ticket necessary to enter Seven Mile Beach. It is a public beach freely accessible to everyone. As for fees and reductions, there are no special costs for accessing the beach itself. However, rental costs may apply for beach chairs, umbrellas, and water sports equipment, which may be purchased from rental firms positioned along the beach.

Discount: While there may not be explicit discounts for students or seniors, certain rental firms and beach side establishments may offer special pricing or specials during certain seasons.

Visitor's norms & etiquette: Visitors to Seven Mile Beach are encouraged to adhere to specific norms and etiquette to guarantee a good experience for everyone. This involves protecting the natural environment, avoiding trash, and obeying municipal restrictions on noise and conduct.

Weather and Comfort: The weather in the Cayman Islands is often warm and sunny, making Seven Mile Beach an enticing location throughout the year.

However, it is essential to verify weather predictions and any necessary cautions before coming to guarantee the best comfort and safety.

Photography: It is normally permitted on Seven Mile Beach, although it is essential to be sensitive to other beach-goers' privacy and obtain permission before shooting close-up shots of people.

Personal Review: It is a stunning beach with a crystal blue ocean and nice white sand. There are several restaurants and pubs positioned along the beach, so you can quickly find something to eat or drink. There is also a range of water sports activities accessible, such as swimming, sunbathing, snorkeling, and jet skiing.

Cayman Turtle Centre: A Sea Turtle Experience

Located on Grand Cayman, the Cayman Turtle Centre provides a unique and participatory sea turtle experience that is appreciated by residents and tourists alike. It is one of the Cayman Islands' most popular attractions, allowing a chance to learn about and interact with these wonderful animals.

The Cayman Turtle Centre is not just a tourism site but also a conservation and research center committed to the protection of sea turtles. It acts as a refuge for many types of turtles, notably the endangered green sea turtle. Visitors may observe the full life cycle of these remarkable species, from hatchlings to adults, and learn about the center's work to preserve and rehabilitate them.

One of the features of the Cayman Turtle Centre is the touch tanks, where visitors can get up close and personal with newborn turtles. This hands-on experience enables people to handle and interact with these charming critters under the care of expert personnel.

For those wanting an even more immersive experience, the facility gives the option to swim and dive with turtles in a vast saltwater lagoon. This unusual meeting gives a new viewpoint on these lovely animals in their native surroundings.

Beyond the turtles, the Cayman Turtle Centre also provides additional attractions and activities. Visitors may explore the nature path, which highlights the rich flora and animals of the Cayman Islands. The park is also home to unique birds, crocodiles, and other local fauna, making it a fascinating experience for nature fans.

The center features educational lectures and interactive displays, presenting insights into the life cycle, biology, and conservation activities around sea turtles. Visitors may learn about the challenges confronting these amazing species and how they can help their preservation and conservation.

In terms of facilities, the Cayman Turtle Centre provides amenities such as restaurants, gift stores, and picnic spots, assuring a pleasant and pleasurable visit for everybody. The facility is conveniently accessible and welcomes guests of all ages, making it an excellent family-friendly destination.

As a popular tourist location, it's crucial to understand that the Cayman Turtle Centre charges an entrance price for access. The charge may vary, therefore it's suggested to check the official website or call the facility for the most up-to-date pricing information.

Extra Information on The Cayman Turtle Centre:

Location: The Cayman Turtle Centre is situated in West Bay, Grand Cayman.

Opening and closing hours: The Cayman Turtle Centre is open from 9 am to 4:30 pm, seven days a week.

Accessibility: The Cayman Turtle Centre is wheelchair accessible. There is a ramp going up to the entrance, and the facility is on one level.

Admission charge: The admission fee for the Cayman Turtle Centre is $18 for adults, $12 for children ages 4-12, and free for children under 4.

Discounts: There are discounts for students and elders. Students with valid IDs may get in for $12, and seniors (65+) can get in for $15.

Online tickets: There is an online ticketing option for the Cayman Turtle Centre. Tickets may be obtained on the center's website.

Visitors' norms & etiquettes: Visitors are urged to be courteous of the turtles and the center's amenities. No smoking, drinking, or feeding of the turtles is permitted. Visitors are also requested to remain on the pathways and not touch the turtles.

Weather and comfort: The weather in Grand Cayman is pleasant and sunny year-round. Visitors should wear comfortable shoes and sunscreen.

Photography: Photography is permitted at the Cayman Turtle Centre. However, flash photography is not permitted within the turtle ponds.

Personal review: It is an excellent location to learn about sea turtles and their protection. I also relished seeing the turtles up close and personal.

Stingray City: Swimming with Friendly Rays

Stingray City is an outstanding and unique sight that has won the hearts of tourists to the Cayman Islands. Located in the North Sound of Grand Cayman, it is a shallow sandbar where tourists may engage and swim with gentle southern stingrays in their native environment.

Stingray City is recognized internationally for its unique chance to get up close and personal with these fascinating aquatic critters. These gigantic animals, varying in size from a few feet to several feet in wingspan, glide gently across the pure turquoise waters, offering an amazing experience.

The site's appeal may be linked to the friendly and docile character of the stingrays, making it safe and ideal for visitors of all ages.

As you wade into the waist-deep water, you'll be met by these inquisitive and friendly animals, ready to connect and even be hand-fed by visitors. These lovely animals are recognized for their loving demeanor and sensitive dispositions, offering a genuinely spectacular encounter. Trained guides accompany tourists, imparting information and guaranteeing a safe and enjoyable interaction.

You'll get the ability to touch, feed, and even hold these delicate animals as they gently glide through the water. Don't be shocked if they rub against your legs, since they have gotten used to human presence and contact. It's a surreal sensation to be in such close contact with these gorgeous aquatic animals.

The appeal of Stingray City rests not only in the encounter with the rays but also in the gorgeous surroundings. The crystal-clear seas, blue sky, and panoramic vistas form a beautiful setting for this incredible journey.

While Stingray City is a hugely popular attraction, it's necessary to emphasize the well-being of the rays and the preservation of their natural habitat. Visitors are advised to handle the stingrays with respect, following the directions set by the guides. This offers a sustainable and eco-friendly experience for everyone engaged.

Extra information on Stingray City:

Location: Stingray City is a sandbar situated in the North Sound of Grand Cayman, roughly a 20-minute boat journey from Seven Mile Beach.

Opening and closing hours: Stingray City is open 24 hours a day, 7 days a week. However, most trips run from 9 am to 3 pm.

Accessibility: Stingray City is wheelchair accessible. Steps are going down to the sandbar, and there are also wheelchair-accessible boats available for cruises.

Admission charge: There is no admission fee to Stingray City. However, there is a price for trips, which normally runs from $25 to $40 per person.

Discounts: There are discounts for students and elders on various tours.

Visitors' guidelines & etiquettes: Visitors are urged to be courteous of the stingrays and their surroundings. No smoking, drinking, or feeding the stingrays is permitted.
Visitors are also requested to remain on the sandbar and not touch the stingrays' tails.

Weather and comfort: The weather in Grand Cayman is pleasant and sunny year-round. Visitors should wear comfortable beachwear and sunscreen.

Photography: Photography is permitted in Stingray City. However, flash photography is not permitted near stingrays.

Personal review: It was a unique and wonderful experience to swim among the stingrays. The stingrays were friendly and interesting, and it was incredible to see them up close.

Here are some helpful ideas for visiting Stingray City:

1. Wear water shoes to protect your feet from the sand and pebbles.
2. Bring a towel to dry off after swimming.
3. Bring sunscreen and a hat to protect yourself from the sun.
4. Be patient and courteous to the stingrays.
5. Have fun!

Pedro St. James National Historic Site: The Birthplace of Democracy

Pedro St. James National Historic Site, regarded as the "Birthplace of Democracy," occupies a major place in the history of the Cayman Islands.

This majestic mansion, situated on the southern shore of Majestic Cayman, serves as a symbol of freedom, democracy, and national pride.

The site is noteworthy for being the venue where the Cayman Islands' first elected parliament assembly took place in 1831. This momentous event marked the beginning of the islands' democratic path and entrenched Pedro St. James as a cornerstone of Caymanian identity.

Visitors at Pedro St. James may visit the wonderfully restored Great House, a towering two-story edifice that gives an insight into the past. Inside, interactive displays and multimedia presentations bring the history of the Cayman Islands to life, illustrating the hardships, achievements, and resilience of its people.

The adjacent gardens of Pedro St. James are similarly intriguing. Lush gardens, breathtaking vistas of the Caribbean Sea, and calm walks create a serene backdrop for tourists to immerse themselves in the natural beauty of the island.

The property also contains a theater that presents instructional films about the history and culture of the Cayman Islands. Additionally, guests may have a meal or snack at the on-site restaurant, which provides wonderful views of the surrounding environment.

Pedro St. James National Historic Site serves as a beacon of cultural heritage and a tribute to the necessity of preserving the Cayman Islands' past.

It is a must-visit place for people interested in learning about the beginnings of democracy in the area and acquiring a greater knowledge of the Caymanian character.

Extra Information about Pedro St. James National Historic Site:

Location: Pedro St. James National Historic Site is situated in Bodden Town, Grand Cayman, Cayman Islands.

Opening and closing hours: Pedro St. James is open from 9 am to 5 pm, seven days a week.

Accessibility: Pedro St. James is wheelchair accessible. There is a ramp going up to the entrance, and the grounds are level.

Admission charge: There is an admission fee of $15 for adults, $10 for children ages 5-12, and free for children under 5.

Discounts: There is a discount for students and elders. Students with valid IDs may get in for $10, while seniors (65+) can get in for $12.50.

Online tickets: There is no online ticketing option for Pedro St. James. Tickets must be bought on the spot.

Visitors' norms and etiquettes: Visitors are urged to be respectful of the property and its surroundings. No smoking, drinking, or trash is permitted. Visitors are also requested to remain on the trails and not climb on the walls.

Weather and comfort: The weather in Grand Cayman is pleasant and sunny year-round. Visitors should wear comfortable shoes and sunscreen.

Photography: Photography is permitted at Pedro St. James. However, flash photography is not permitted within the Great House.

Personal review: It is a lovely location with a lot of history. The Great House is very beautiful, and it is fascinating to read about the role that Pedro St. James had in Caymanian history.

Here are some of the positive and negative qualities of Pedro St. James National Historic Site:

PROS

1. The Great House is a gorgeous and historic edifice.
2. The facility is well-maintained and simple to navigate.
3. There are a range of exhibitions and activities to learn about Caymanian history.
4. The property is placed in a wonderful location with spectacular views.

CONS

1. The venue may be congested, particularly during the high tourist season.
2. The displays are not usually well-labeled or explained.
3. Some of the activities, such as the guided excursions, might be pricey.

Overall, I believe Pedro St. James National Historic Site is a great visit for anybody interested in Caymanian history or architecture.

NTAMED BEAUTY CAYMAN BRAC

CHAPTER 4

Introduction to Cayman Brac

Welcome to the intriguing island of Cayman Brac, a hidden treasure waiting to be discovered. In this chapter, we will take you on a tour to find the delights of Cayman Brac, a smaller but equally charming sister island of Grand Cayman.

Cayman Brac is situated roughly 90 miles northeast of Grand Cayman and is noted for its particular charm and natural beauty. The island receives its name from the large limestone bluff, or "brac" in Gaelic, that extends along its eastern shore. This geological wonder not only gives spectacular panoramic views but also offers an assortment of outdoor experiences for nature aficionados and thrill-seekers.

As you set foot on Cayman Brac, you'll be welcomed by spectacular panoramas of rugged limestone cliffs that rise majestically from the blue ocean.
This rough environment offers the ideal background for outdoor excursions and exploration. Lace up your hiking boots and tour the island's well-maintained paths, taking you to isolated coves, secret caverns, and panoramic overlooks. Don't forget to bring your camera to capture the awe-inspiring natural treasures that greet you.

Beyond its natural beauty, Cayman Brac is also immersed in rich cultural traditions. Engage with the welcoming inhabitants and immerse yourself in the island's traditions and customs. Discover the craft of thatch weaving, a talent handed down through generations, and watch the construction of exquisite baskets and hats. Indulge in the island's gastronomic wonders, eating freshly caught fish and traditional Caymanian delicacies that will excite your taste buds.

Uncovering Cayman Brac is an invitation to unearth the island's hidden gems. Dive into crystal-clear seas filled with vivid marine life, discover enigmatic shipwrecks, and engage in snorkeling or scuba diving activities that will leave you in awe of the undersea delights. For adrenaline lovers, the island provides exhilarating rock climbing options and the opportunity to tackle the legendary Brac Bluff.

Whether you seek leisure on gorgeous beaches, want adventure in the great outdoors, or wish to connect with the local culture, Cayman Brac delivers a unique experience. So, gather your sense of adventure and get ready to unearth the mysteries of this enchanting island, where every discovery uncovers a new chapter in your Cayman Islands experience.

Brac Reef Beach

Brac Reef Beach, situated on the southern shore of Cayman Brac, has a rich history that stretches back to the early colonization of the Cayman Islands. The beach receives its name from the surrounding region, known as "The Brac," which alludes to the rough limestone cliffs that define the island.

In the past, Brac Reef Beach was mostly frequented by local fishermen who depended on the rich seas for their livelihood. It functioned as a center for fishing activities and a meeting spot for the community. Over time, as tourism expanded in the Cayman Islands, Brac Reef Beach became famous for its natural beauty and unspoiled surroundings, bringing people from across the globe. Today, Brac Reef Beach is a popular location for both visitors and locals alike. It serves as a symbol of the island's natural beauty and the significance of protecting its pristine shoreline.

As I stood on the sands of Brac Reef Beach, I couldn't help but experience a feeling of amazement and wonder. The smooth white sand tickled my toes, and the calm wind stroked my face, inviting me to this gorgeous bit of heaven. It felt as if time had stopped still, enabling me to absorb myself in the rich history and natural beauty that surrounded me.

As I learned about the beach's history, I couldn't help but imagine the local fisherman who formerly depended on its plentiful seas. Their tales came to life in my head, presenting a vivid image of a bustling community centered around the water. The echoes of their laughter and the sounds of their boats seemed to linger in the air, reminding me of the beach's modest origins.

Today, Brac Reef Beach endures as a tribute to the island's dedication to conserving its natural treasures. The colorful coral reefs only a short swim away enticed me to investigate their underwater world. Snorkeling among the colorful fish and enchanting marine life was like entering a new dimension, where time slowed down and the troubles of the world slipped away.

Leaving Brac Reef Beach was not easy, since it had caught my heart and left an unforgettable impact on my soul. It represented more than simply a gorgeous length of beach; it encapsulated the soul of the Cayman Islands, with its rich history, pristine shoreline, and welcoming hospitality.

For those wanting an intimate experience with nature's magnificence and a look into the island's history, Brac Reef Beach is a place that shouldn't be missed. It encourages you to walk into a realm of wonder and calm, where time appears to slow down and the beauty of the Caribbean unfolds before your eyes.

Aside from Brac Reef Beach, Cayman Brac is home to numerous additional magnificent beaches, each giving its distinct charm and attractiveness.

Here are a few prominent beaches on the island:

1. Buccaneer Beach: Buccaneer Beach, also known as Buccaneer's Landing, is a picturesque beach situated on the western extremity of the island.
It has soft sand, shallow waves, and a pleasant wind, making it a favorite destination for families and beach enthusiasts. The beach also provides picnic tables and shade for those seeking to enjoy a relaxing day by the surf.

2. West Extremity Beach: Situated on the western extremity of Cayman Brac, West End Beach is recognized for its rocky coastline and rugged beauty. It provides a dramatic background for magnificent sunsets and gives possibilities for beachcombing and exploring the tidal pools produced by the natural granite formations.

3. Pollard Bay Beach: Nestled on the northwestern edge of the island, Pollard Bay Beach is a serene and private place. Its rocky coastline, coupled with sandy spots, produces a unique terrain that is great for beachcombing and soaking in the picturesque grandeur of the surrounding cliffs.

4. Charlie's Reef: Charlie's Reef is a hidden treasure buried away on the southern shore of Cayman Brac. While it may not have a sandy beach, it is recognized for its great snorkeling and diving options. The shallow, crystal-clear waters teem with beautiful coral reefs and a plethora of marine life, delivering an exciting underwater excursion.

5. Owen Island Beach: Accessible through a short boat trip from Cayman Brac, Owen Island Beach is a quiet haven. This tiny, isolated island features gorgeous white dunes and turquoise seas, giving a quiet getaway from the rush and bustle of everyday life.

6. Lighthouse Beach: Lighthouse Beach, as the name implies, is situated near the lighthouse on the southeastern point of the island. This distant beach gives a feeling of tranquility and natural beauty. Its craggy coastline, limestone formations, and panoramic views of the Caribbean Sea make a stunning backdrop for exploration or just enjoying the calm.

7. Spot Bay Beach: Spot Bay Beach is a remote beach situated on the western side of Cayman Brac. It provides a tranquil escape and an opportunity to explore the island's natural beauty away from the tourists. The beach boasts smooth sand, quiet seas, and shaded spaces offered by the surrounding trees
.

8. South Side Public Beach: Situated on the southern shore, South Side Public Beach is a favorite meeting location for residents and tourists alike. With its broad expanse of beaches, tranquil waves, and covered picnic places, it's a fantastic destination for a family day out.

The Bluff: Spectacular Views and Hiking Trails

The Bluff Reserve is a 473-hectare (1,170-acre) section of dry woodland on the eastern end of Cayman Brac. It is home to a diversity of plant and animal species, including Cuban Amazon parrots, white-crowned pigeons, and Caribbean elaenia.

This tall limestone cliff, running over the island's length, features an outstanding height that provides tourists with panoramic perspectives of the surrounding blue seas and verdant surroundings. The reserve is also noted for its caverns, which were originally utilized by the island's early occupants for refuge and storage.

The Bluff Reserve is available to the public, and hiking options abound at The Bluff, appealing to explorers of all ability levels.

The routes vary from pleasant strolls to more strenuous excursions, enabling hikers to explore the region at their speed. Each route provides its particular appeal, leading to stunning perspectives of the Caribbean Sea and the Cayman Brac shoreline, and important monuments along the way.

For those desiring a leisurely trek, the Lower Bluff Trail offers a lovely trail through the island's rich greenery, affording sights of exotic bird species and occasional sightings of local fauna. As you rise to the Upper Bluff Trail, the terrain gets rougher, providing you with greater awe-inspiring vistas of the Caribbean Sea.

The difficulty levels vary depending on the selected route, but regardless of the way you take, the fascinating sights and natural beauties will leave you in amazement. Look out for renowned monuments like the Lighthouse, built atop The Bluff, which acts as a guiding light for mariners and gives a magnificent outlook for hikers.

My personal experience at The Bluff was simply remarkable. As I climbed along the paths, I was given stunning sights of the boundless ocean, the craggy coastline, and the beautiful regions below. The sense of success upon reaching the peak and taking in the panoramic vistas was just amazing. The reserve is accessible from 8 am to 4pm every day and there is no admission charge.

Here are some things to bear in mind while visiting the Bluff Reserve:

1. Wear comfortable shoes and attire.
2. Bring water and snacks.
3. Be on the lookout for animals.
4. Leave no trace.

Dive Sites and Snorkeling Spots

With a wealth of diving sites and snorkeling areas to explore, the island provides memorable underwater experiences for all skill levels.

The MV Captain Keith Tibbetts wreck

One of the most popular diving locations is the MV Captain Keith Tibbetts wreck. This 330-feet long Russian ship, sunk purposely in 1996, now lies on the ocean below, enticing divers from across the globe. As you descend into the depths, you'll be welcomed by a breathtaking diversity of marine life, including colorful corals, sponges, and schools of tropical fish.

Here are some crucial data and observations regarding this unique underwater attraction:

Location: The MV Captain Keith Tibbetts wreck is situated off the northern shore of Cayman Brac, near the hamlet of West End.

Opening and Closing Hours: As a diving site, there are no defined opening and closing hours. Diving activities normally take place during daytime hours.

Accessibility & Wheelchair Access: Access to the MV Captain Keith Tibbetts wreck is confined to scuba divers only. Snorkelers may also examine the wreck from the surface. Unfortunately, wheelchair access is not accessible owing to the nature of the underwater habitat.

Admission cost and Tickets: Since the MV Captain Keith Tibbetts wreck is an open diving site, there is normally no admission cost or tickets necessary. However, if you opt to dive with a dive operator, they may charge a fee for their services.

Discounts for Students and Elders: Discount pricing for students and elders may vary based on the diving operator you pick. It is recommended to ask the individual diving operator about any possible discounts.

Online Ticketing Options: Online ticketing options may not be valid for the MV Captain Keith Tibbetts wreck since it is not a ticketed attraction. However, you may arrange diving excursions and packages with dive companies online.

Visitors Rules and Etiquettes: It is necessary to use appropriate diving methods and respect the marine environment while visiting the wreck. Adhere follow the rules supplied by your dive operator and always emphasize safety. Avoid touching or injuring the coral or aquatic life, and be attentive to your surroundings to avoid any disruptions.

Weather and Comfort: guarantee you have adequate diving gear and apparel to guarantee comfort and safety throughout your dive.

Photography: Photography is normally permitted at the MV Captain Keith Tibbetts wreck. Capture magnificent underwater photographs of the wreck and the aquatic life, but remember to be careful and avoid damaging the environment or harming yourself or others.

Personal Review: Well, I didn't dive in, but my husband being a keen diver, flexed the MV Captain Keith Tibbetts wreck, which was a great experience for him. The wreck's towering appearance and the aquatic life that has made it their home make a compelling underwater landscape. Swimming beside the wreck's structure and observing its transition into an artificial reef was simply awe-inspiring.

Cayman Brac Wall

For those seeking unusual underwater formations, the iconic Cayman Brac Wall is a must-visit. The Cayman Brac Wall, a world-renowned diving location, provides an amazing underwater experience in Cayman Brac.

Location: Located off the shore of the island, this magnificent underwater cliff shows beautiful coral formations and plenty of aquatic life.
This stunning underwater cliff lowers to astonishing depths, displaying fascinating coral formations, fissures, and swim-throughs. The vertical wall teems with marine life, including reef sharks, turtles, and a variety of fish species.

Opening and Closing Hours: As a natural diving site, the Cayman Brac Wall does not have fixed opening and closing hours. Divers have the option to explore this location at their leisure, assuming they comply with safety requirements and proper weather conditions.

Accessibility & Wheelchair Access: Accessibility to the Cayman Brac Wall is mostly via boat, with local diving companies providing guided tours. While wheelchair access may be restricted on certain boats, it's advisable to consult with the diving operators for particular accommodations.

Admission cost and Tickets: There is no admission charge or ticket necessary to enter the Cayman Brac Wall. Divers will normally pay for diving packages or individual dives, with rates varying among various dive companies. As of 2023, the prices may vary from $80 to $150 for each dive, depending on variables like equipment rental and extra services.

Discounts for Students and Elders: Discount prices for students or seniors may be available, however, it's essential to check with the diving operators for any special pricing choices or promotions. Some diving companies provide online ticketing alternatives, enabling divers to schedule their dives in advance. This may give convenience and assure supply, especially during high seasons.

Visitors Rules and Etiquettes: Visitors to the Cayman Brac Wall are obliged to obey diving regulations and etiquette. This involves diving within their certification restrictions, preserving marine life and coral formations, and maintaining proper buoyancy control to prevent hurting the environment. Safety standards, such as diving buddy systems, should be followed at all times.

Weather and Comfort: Weather conditions and comfort levels may vary, so it's essential to check local predictions and talk with dive operators for the most acceptable diving periods. The mild tropical environment of Cayman Brac affords good water temperatures throughout the year, enabling suitable diving conditions.

Photography: Photography is normally permitted at the Cayman Brac Wall, however, it's vital to take care and prevent upsetting marine life or damage to the coral. Underwater photographers will find enough possibilities to capture the splendor of the wall's bright coral formations and the rich underwater ecology.

Personal Review: I strongly suggest visiting the Cayman Brac Wall for its spectacular beauty and the opportunity to discover the marvels of the underwater world.

Coral Gardens

Snorkelers will discover a variety of clean areas to explore, such as the Coral Gardens. This shallow reef region provides crystal-clear waters packed with beautiful coral formations and a kaleidoscope of tropical species. It's a wonderful site for snorkelers of all ages and experience levels to view the beauty of the underwater world.

Here's everything you need to know about this interesting location:

Location: Coral Gardens is situated along the southern shore of Cayman Brac, readily accessible from many spots on the island.

Opening and Closing Hours: There are no particular opening and closing hours for Coral Gardens since it is a natural site available for exploring at any time.

Accessibility & Wheelchair Access: The snorkeling area is accessible to tourists of all abilities, with roads and entrance points intended to facilitate wheelchair access.

Admission Charge or Ticket: There is no admission charge or ticket necessary to visit Coral Gardens. It is a public snorkeling location freely available to all guests. As there is no admission price, there are no particular discount rates for students or elders.

Visitors Rules and Etiquettes: When visiting Coral Gardens, it is vital to observe basic measures to conserve the sensitive marine habitat. Avoid standing or touching coral formations, since they are delicate and may be easily harmed. Refrain from feeding or pursuing marine animals, since it interrupts their normal behavior. Take just images and leave only footprints, respecting the environment and leaving it as you found it.

Weather and Comfort: The weather on Cayman Brac is often warm and tropical, giving suitable conditions for snorkeling at Coral Gardens. It is essential to check the weather prediction before venturing out and to wear suitable sun protection and swimsuits for a pleasant experience.

Photography: Photography is permitted at Coral Gardens, allowing a chance to capture the beauty of the underwater environment. Remember to protect marine life and coral structures, maintaining a safe distance when shooting images.

Personal Review: Coral Gardens is a great jewel for snorkeling aficionados. As I submerged myself in the crystal-clear waters, I was enthralled by the kaleidoscope of hues that opened under the surface. It was a thrill to meet schools of tropical fish, beautiful sea turtles, and even the rare stingray swimming past.

Buccaneer's Reef

Another famous snorkeling area is the Buccaneer's Reef. Located near Buccaneer's Beach, this shallow reef has a wealth of marine life, including friendly stingrays and lively sergeant majors. Snorkelers may gently explore the reef, marveling at the vivid coral gardens and seeing the colorful fish dashing through the water.

Here's all you need to know about this magnificent spot:

Location: Buccaneer's Reef is located on the western side of Cayman Brac, readily accessible from many spots on the island.

Accessibility & Wheelchair Access: Buccaneer's Reef is accessible for snorkeling throughout the day, enabling guests to appreciate its beauty at their leisure.

The snorkeling area may require some walking over rough terrain, but it is normally accessible to most guests. Unfortunately, wheelchair access may be restricted owing to the natural terrain.

Admission Charge or Ticket: There is no special admission charge for reaching Buccaneer's Reef. It is a public snorkeling location open for everyone to enjoy free of charge.

Visitors Rules and Etiquettes: To maintain the sustainability of the reef and the protection of marine animals, it is vital to adhere to proper snorkeling practices. Avoid touching or injuring the coral, remain a safe distance from aquatic wildlife, and stop littering. Respect fellow snorkelers and promote a pleasant and tranquil atmosphere.

Photography: Photography is normally permitted at Buccaneer's Reef, enabling you to capture the magnificent underwater environment and marine life. However, it is crucial to be cautious of your surroundings and preserve the maritime environment when shooting images.

Cayman Brac's diving locations and snorkeling areas serve both beginners and expert divers and snorkelers. Local diving operators provide guided trips, assuring a safe and engaging experience for everybody.

Rock Iguanas Sanctuary

The Rock Iguanas Sanctuary in the Cayman Islands has a long history related to the protection of the endangered Rock Iguanas. These rare reptiles have inhabited the islands for generations, but their population suffered significant challenges owing to habitat loss and human activity.

Recognizing the need to safeguard these amazing animals, the Cayman Islands government created the Rock Iguanas Sanctuary. The sanctuary serves as a designated location for the preservation and protection of the Rock Iguanas, providing them with a secure home to develop and breed.

Through coordinated efforts between conservation groups, local communities, and government agencies, the refuge has been vital in protecting the iguanas' population. It provides a regulated and monitored habitat that enables the study of their behavior, breeding habits, and ecological demands.

The sanctuary's principal purpose is to safeguard the Rock Iguanas and their natural environment, guaranteeing their survival for future generations. It plays a critical role in increasing awareness about the significance of maintaining these rare reptiles, not merely for their intrinsic worth but also the overall ecological balance of the Cayman Islands.

Today, the Rock Iguanas Sanctuary remains a symbol of the Cayman Islands' dedication to wildlife preservation. It acts as an educational resource, involving visitors in learning about the iguanas' biology, the challenges they face, and continuing conservation efforts. The refuge also actively supports research activities aimed at better understanding and safeguarding these vulnerable reptiles.

Here are a few things to note:

Opening and Closing Hours: The sanctuary works from Monday through Saturday, with opening hours from 9:00 AM to 4:00 PM. It is closed on Sundays and public holidays.

Accessibility & Wheelchair Access: In terms of accessibility, the sanctuary is built to accommodate guests of varying mobility levels. Wheelchair access is offered, ensuring that everyone may enjoy the event.

Admission Charge or Ticket: To access the Rock Iguanas Sanctuary, there is an admission charge of $10 per person. However, it's crucial to check for any updates or changes in the costs before your visit.

Discount Rates: Discount rates for students and elders may be provided, giving lower admission prices. It is essential to enquire about these reductions and offer appropriate identification when buying your tickets.

Visitors Rules and Etiquettes: When visiting the Rock Iguanas Sanctuary, there are particular norms and etiquettes to obey. Respect the iguanas' natural environment and keep a safe distance to prevent creating any disruption. Follow the instruction of the sanctuary workers and remain on designated routes to conserve the delicate ecology.

Weather and Comfort: As for weather and comfort, it's essential to examine the local weather conditions before your visit. Wear suitable footwear and attire for outdoor activities, since you may be exploring natural paths and rough terrains.

Photography: Photography is normally permitted at the Rock Iguanas Sanctuary, but it's vital to be sensitive to the iguanas' well-being and avoid using flash, which may shock or damage them. Capture the beauty of the sanctuary and its residents while respecting their natural behavior.

Personal Review: My evaluation of the Rock Iguanas Sanctuary is incredibly good. It gives a rare chance to watch these interesting reptiles in their native surroundings.

chapter five

DISCOVERING
LITTLE CAYMAN

Introduction to Little Cayman

Welcome to Little Cayman, a hidden jewel in the Caribbean that provides a wonderful vacation for first-time visitors. Nestled in the Cayman Islands, this calm and untouched island is a retreat for nature enthusiasts, adventure seekers, and those seeking tranquility.

Little Cayman is the smallest of the three Cayman Islands, famed for its pure white sandy beaches, crystal-clear turquoise seas, and rich marine life. With a population of only approximately 200 inhabitants, it emanates a laid-back and intimate environment, making it the ideal place for anyone seeking a calm vacation.

This lovely island is recognized for its world-class diving and snorkeling possibilities.

The Bloody Bay Marine Park, a protected marine reserve, includes vivid coral reefs, underwater caverns, and a wide variety of marine creatures, including colorful tropical fish, sea turtles, and stingrays. Dive enthusiasts may visit notable dive locations like the Bloody Bay Wall, a vertical coral wall that plunges to depths of nearly 1,800 meters, affording magnificent underwater panoramas.

Aside from its underwater delights, Little Cayman is also a sanctuary for birdwatchers and wildlife aficionados. The island is home to the Booby Pond Nature Reserve, a haven for the endangered red-footed booby birds. Visitors may observe these amazing seabirds breeding and fly across the skies, delivering a unique and fascinating experience.

When it comes to lodgings, Little Cayman provides a selection of attractive and tiny beachside resorts and comfortable guesthouses.

These lodgings merge harmoniously with the island's natural splendor, delivering a calm and immersive experience.

Whether you spend your days lazing on isolated beaches, discovering underwater marvels, or immersing yourself in the island's pristine environment, Little Cayman provides a revitalizing and unique experience for first-time guests. Get ready to go on a voyage to this paradise uncovered and experience the genuine essence of leisure, natural beauty, and tranquility that await you on Little Cayman.

Booby Pond Nature Reserve: Bird-watching Haven

Booby Pond Nature Reserve, situated in Little Cayman, is a charming refuge noted for its rich birds and magnificent natural beauty. The reserve's history is founded on the attempts to safeguard the unique ecology and the different bird species that depend on it.

Established in 1994, Booby Pond Nature Reserve was developed with the main objective of conserving the breeding habitats of the Red-footed Booby, a spectacular seabird species. This location became identified as one of the biggest and most significant nesting grounds for Red-footed Boobies in the Caribbean. The reserve comprises roughly 200 acres, containing coastal marshes, lagoons, mangrove forests, and unspoiled beaches.

Booby Pond Nature Reserve retains tremendous value as a sanctuary for both resident and migratory birds. It is home to an incredible assortment of avian species, including the Red-footed Booby, Brown Booby, West Indian Whistling Duck, herons, egrets, and a broad range of migratory birds. The reserve's various ecosystems offer crucial feeding, breeding, and resting grounds for these species, making it a critical conservation location.

Today, Booby Pond Nature Reserve serves as a key location for scientific study, monitoring, and conservation initiatives. Scientists and bird lovers research the behavior, ecology, and population dynamics of permanent and visiting bird species. Their results give significant insights into the general health of the ecosystem and influence conservation initiatives to safeguard these unique birds.

The reserve also plays a key role in increasing awareness and supporting environmental education. Visitors have the chance to tour the reserve's pathways and observation platforms, where they may watch the birds in their natural environment and learn about the need of protecting their delicate habitats. Guided tours and educational activities further improve the tourist experience and promote a greater knowledge of the critical role that bird conservation plays in preserving a healthy and vibrant ecosystem.

A few things to note:

Booby Pond Nature Reserve is located on the south side of Little Cayman, covering a wide wetland region and coastal ecosystems. The reserve is accessible every day from dawn to sunset, offering visitors sufficient opportunity to enjoy its natural marvels. The reserve features accessible walkways and boardwalks, ensuring that persons with mobility issues may enjoy the beauty of the region.

As of 2023, there is a modest admission charge to reach Booby Pond Nature Reserve. The charge pays for the conservation efforts and management of the reserve.

Discounts for students and elders may be available, so it's worth enquiring about any concession pricing. While online ticketing alternatives may not be available for Booby Pond Nature Reserve, you may normally buy your admission ticket upon arrival to the reserve.

To preserve the preservation of the sensitive environment and the well-being of the species, it is vital to follow the authorized routes and comply with any notice or directions offered.

Visitors are asked to remain on specified routes, abstain from disturbing the animals, and avoid littering. Respecting the natural environment and adopting responsible tourism enriches everyone's experience.

The weather in Little Cayman is often warm and pleasant, with cooling sea breezes. It is advised to dress comfortably, use adequate footwear for walking, and apply sunscreen and bug repellent. It's also a good idea to carry a hat, sunglasses, and a water bottle to remain hydrated.

Booby Pond Nature Reserve gives a fantastic opportunity for photography, capturing rare bird species and breathtaking surroundings. However, it's crucial to be respectful of the animals and their habitats. Avoid coming too near to nesting locations or upsetting the birds. Always observe any special restrictions for photography to minimize any possible influence on the environment.

Personal Review: The reserve's stunning vistas and various bird species provide a great birding experience. Despite the occasional obstacles of uncertain weather and insects, the well-maintained pathways and accessible boardwalks made exploring straightforward. The ability to witness unusual birds in their native environment made the additional admission charge worthwhile.

Point of Sand Beach: Secluded Paradise

Point of Sand Beach in Little Cayman is a hidden treasure that bears a rich history and is a secluded paradise to this day. Located on the easternmost extremity of the island, this beautiful length of sandy beach has captured travelers with its natural beauty and calm environment.

In the past, Point of Sand Beach functioned as a meeting location for people and a haven of consolation for fishermen seeking relief after hard days at sea. Its distant position and pristine environs made it a valued getaway for individuals who sought solitude and connection with nature.

Over time, knowledge of Point of Sand Beach's natural grandeur spread, drawing daring visitors and nature lovers from across the globe. Its image as a quiet paradise spread, and it became a desirable resort for people seeking an escape from the hectic world.

Today, Point of Sand Beach remains a symbol of unadulterated natural beauty and a tribute to the preservation of Little Cayman's pristine shoreline. The beach remains free from commercial development, keeping its unspoiled appeal and affording guests a taste of paradise.

Visitors to Point of Sand Beach may bask in the warm Caribbean sun, walk along the powdered white sands, and take in the spectacular views of the crystal-clear blue seas. The solitude of the beach creates a feeling of calm and retreat, enabling guests to immerse themselves in the serene beauty of their surroundings.

As you stroll down the coast, you may meet rich marine life, including colorful fish and inquisitive sea turtles. The beach is also a popular site for snorkeling and diving, where you can explore the vivid coral reefs close offshore and discover the wonderful undersea life that flourishes in these sheltered waters.
Point of Sand Beach serves as a tribute to the necessity of maintaining natural landscapes and the beauty of unspoiled coastlines. It serves as a reminder that even in our contemporary world, there are still secret havens where nature reigns supreme, allowing us to reconnect with its beauties and find consolation in its embrace.

A few things to note:

Point of Sand Beach is situated on the eastern edge of Little Cayman, a quiet island in the Cayman Islands. The Beach is available to tourists throughout the day since there are no fixed opening or closing hours.

The beach is accessible by road, and there are parking facilities available nearby. However, it's vital to know that the ground going to the beach may be hilly and sandy, which might cause issues with wheelchair access.

Point of Sand Beach is a public beach, and there is no admission charge or ticket necessary to use it. Visitors may enjoy its natural beauty freely.

While enjoying Point of Sand Beach, it's vital to adhere to specific norms and etiquette to protect its natural beauty. These include avoiding trash, respecting the environment and animals, and leaving the beach as you found it. Additionally, it is important to observe any posted warnings or instructions for safety considerations.

The weather in the Cayman Islands is often warm and tropical, offering suitable conditions for beachgoers. It's important to check the weather forecast before visiting Point of Sand Beach to have a nice experience.
Don't forget to pack UV protection, such as sunscreen, hats, and sunglasses, as well as plenty of drinking water to remain hydrated.

Photography is permitted and encouraged at Point of Sand Beach. The gorgeous surroundings give amazing possibilities to capture the splendor of the beach, its turquoise waves, and magnificent vistas. Remember to be polite to people and sensitive to their privacy while shooting images.

Personal Review: My visit to Point of Sand Beach was a mixed experience, including both pleasant and bad features. On the bright side, the beach's quiet position and unspoiled natural beauty were very appealing. The silky white dunes and crystal-clear seas formed a lovely scene that was great for relaxation and solitude.

However, I must agree that reaching the beach was a little tough. The rocky and sandy terrain going to the beach made it difficult to travel, particularly for persons with mobility impairments or those using a wheelchair. It would be good if there were better accessibility choices and infrastructure in place to accommodate all guests.

Another feature that attracted my notice was the absence of facilities and services at the beach. While this contributed to the beach's quiet appeal, it also meant that there were no facilities, showers, or food sellers nearby. It's crucial to arrive prepared with your supplies, including water, food, and beach basics.

Despite these little shortcomings, Point of Sand Beach gave me a tranquil and peaceful setting that enabled me to escape from the outer world and connect with nature. The stunning views, particularly from the upper overlooks, made it worth the effort to reach the beach. The lack of an admission charge was also a wonderful surprise, as it enabled everyone to enjoy the beauty of the beach without any financial strain.

Overall, I would suggest visiting Point of Sand Beach if you are looking for a private haven away from the throng. Just be prepared for the hassles of reaching the beach and carry everything you need for a nice stay.

Bloody Bay Marine Park: Underwater Wonders

Bloody Bay Marine Park, situated off the shore of Little Cayman Island, is a famous marine protected area that is known for its spectacular underwater delights. The history of Bloody Bay Marine Park stretches back to the 1980s when the Cayman Islands government realized the need to maintain and safeguard the sensitive marine habitat around the region.

The park's name, Bloody Bay, is derived from the red-colored algae that periodically bloom in the water, providing a vibrant and appealing picture. The park contains a large region of beautiful coral reefs, rich marine life, and magnificent underwater scenery.

The formation of Bloody Bay Marine Park was a crucial step towards protecting the natural beauty and biodiversity of the area. It serves as a haven for a diversity of marine creatures, including beautiful coral formations, tropical fish, sea turtles, rays, and even the odd glimpse of magnificent whale sharks.

Today, Bloody Bay Marine Park is not only a haven for marine life but also a popular destination for divers and snorkelers from throughout the globe. Its pure waters and healthy coral reefs give an unmatched diving experience, with superb visibility and a plethora of marine animals to encounter.

The park serves as a tribute to the dedication of the Cayman Islands to maintaining its natural resources and fostering sustainable tourism. It acts as an educational center, promoting awareness about marine conservation and the need of protecting delicate habitats.

Visitors to Bloody Bay Aquatic Park are asked to adhere to appropriate diving techniques, such as avoiding harming or disturbing aquatic life, respecting the coral reefs, and properly disposing of any trash. By practicing responsible tourism, tourists help the continuing conservation and preservation of this amazing marine habitat.

A few things to note:

Bloody Bay Marine Park is located on the northwest coast of Little Cayman, conveniently accessible from numerous resorts and hotels on the island. The marine park is open year-round for tourists. As it is a natural maritime habitat, there are no defined opening and closing hours.

The maritime park is mostly visited by boat, and there may be limited disability accessibility on particular boats. It is suggested to consult with local tour companies for wheelchair access. Some diving operators or tour firms may offer reduced pricing for students or elders. It is recommended to check with individual operators for any possible discounts.

There is no admission charge to reach Bloody Bay, Marine Park. However, visitors may need to schedule guided tours or excursions with approved diving operators or tour companies, which may require expenses.

Visitors Bloody Bay Marine Park are asked to observe strict laws and procedures to conserve vulnerable marine habitats. This includes not harming or removing any marine creatures, avoiding standing or resting on coral reefs, and wearing reef-friendly sunscreens to limit environmental effects.

The weather in the Cayman Islands is often warm and tropical throughout the year.

Visitors should consider wearing suitable apparel, such as swimsuits and lightweight clothing, and carrying sun protection, like caps and sunscreen.

Photography is typically permitted and encouraged at Bloody Bay Marine Park. However, it is crucial to be conscious of the maritime environment and to avoid creating any disruption or harm to the coral reefs or marine life.

The clarity was amazing, allowing for remarkable encounters with sea turtles, tropical fish, and even the rare eagle ray. The experienced and knowledgeable dive operators delivered a safe and fun experience. However, it is vital to know that weather conditions may occasionally hinder dive and snorkel expeditions, so it is best to plan appropriately.

Owen Island: A Hidden Gem

Owen Island, frequently referred to as "A Hidden Gem," is a small, deserted island situated off the coast of Little Cayman in the Cayman Islands. Despite its modest size, Owen Island boasts a rich history and has become a symbol of natural beauty and preservation.

Originally called "Tibbetts Island," the island was renamed in honor of the famed local boat builder, Mr. Owen, who exploited the island as a supply of lumber for his ships. Over time, Owen Island earned a reputation for its beautiful beaches, blue oceans, and undisturbed natural scenery.

Today, Owen Island exists as a refuge of unspoiled beauty. It remains deserted and undisturbed by human activity, retaining its natural beauty. The island is recognized for its gorgeous sandy beaches, surrounded by colorful coral reefs rich with aquatic life.

Visitors to Owen Island may bask in the peacefulness of its quiet coastlines, experience the undersea marvels via snorkeling or diving, and delight in the beautiful vistas of the Caribbean Sea. It acts as a monument to the necessity of conserving and safeguarding the natural environment.

Owen Island offers a reminder of the unspoiled beauty that exists in the world, and the need to protect and appreciate such natural riches. Its pristine condition serves as a shelter for animals and a testimony to the fragile balance of nature.

While access to Owen Island may be restricted owing to its protected status, visitors to Little Cayman may still appreciate its beauty from a distance, admiring the island as a symbol of the untouched treasures that the Cayman Islands have to offer.

A few things to note:

Owen Island is located off the southern shore of Little Cayman, near the southwestern extremity of the island. As an uninhabited island, Owen Island does not have fixed opening and closing hours. Visitors may normally reach the island throughout the day, however, it's encouraged to arrange your visit during daylight hours for safety and greater visibility.

Access to Owen Island is mostly via boat. The island does not have any dedicated facilities for wheelchair access, and the sandy terrain may provide issues for mobility-impaired persons.

Visitors to Owen Island are urged to observe responsible tourist practices and respect the natural environment. It is crucial to leave no trace, prevent trash, and not damage the flora and animals. Additionally, it is recommended to observe any notice or laws supplied by local authorities. Remember to bring sunscreen, hats, and comfortable clothes for protection from the sun.

Photography is normally permitted on Owen Island. Capture the gorgeous beauty and fauna, but remember to be conscious of the ecosystem and avoid creating any disruption.

The peace and isolation of the island give a retreat from the hectic world. However, it's crucial to remember that being an isolated island, there are no conveniences such as bathroom facilities or amenities accessible. Visitors should plan properly and come equipped with the required materials.

CAYMANIAN DINING AND NIGHTLIFE

Chapter six

As the sun sets over the turquoise seas of the Cayman Islands, a colorful and seductive world of eating and entertainment comes alive. Indulge your taste buds and immerse yourself in the rich tastes, cultural mix, and dynamic environment that Caymanian cuisine and nightlife have to offer. From relishing scrumptious local delicacies to dancing the night away beneath the starlit sky, this chapter encourages you to go on a culinary trip like no other.

Discover a melting pot of culinary influences, where Caribbean spices meet world flare, producing a mix of tastes that will excite your tongue. From freshly caught seafood meals bursting with freshness to traditional Caymanian delicacies handed down through generations, each taste tells a narrative of the island's rich cultural legacy.

But the experience doesn't stop with only the meal. Caymanian nightlife provides a dynamic and exciting atmosphere that caters to all tastes and wants.

Whether you're looking for a laid-back seaside bar, a fashionable cocktail lounge, or a busy nightclub, the possibilities are many. Dance to the rhythm of Caribbean sounds, drink homemade cocktails, and interact with locals and other tourists, making experiences that will last a lifetime.

In this chapter, you will be walked through the culinary jewels and exciting nightlife venues that make the Cayman Islands a refuge for food connoisseurs and night owls alike. From legendary restaurants dishing up exquisite cuisine to secret local treasures off the main path, we will expose the greatest eating and nightlife experiences to guarantee you a unique trip.

So prepare your taste buds, put on your dancing shoes, and get ready to enjoy the tastes, rhythms, and colorful energy of Caymanian cuisine and nightlife.

This chapter promises to take you on a sensory adventure that will leave you hungry for more. Get ready to appreciate every moment and make memories that will last a lifetime.

Caymanian Cuisine and Local Delicacies

When it comes to Caymanian food, prepare yourself for a delectable journey that mixes Caribbean tastes, foreign influences, and a touch of local flair.

At the core of Caymanian cuisine is a fondness for fresh seafood. With the abundance of beautiful seas surrounding the islands, it's no surprise that fish and seafood play a prominent role in many traditional recipes. Indulge in the delicious tastes of locally caught fish like snapper, mahi-mahi, and grouper, served with a range of seasonings and cooking methods that demonstrate the culinary expertise of the island's chefs.

One unique Caymanian meal that cannot be missed is the famed Cayman-style turtle stew. This rich and savory dish pays respect to the island's heritage and traditional culinary origins. Slow-cooked with herbs, spices, and fresh vegetables, the turtle stew offers a real flavor of the Cayman Islands' cultural history.

For those craving a little heat, jerk chicken and pork are must-try foods. Infused with a hot combination of Caribbean spices and slow-cooked to perfection, these meals give a delightful kick that will excite your taste senses. Pair it with traditional sides like rice and peas, plantains, or cassava, and you have a feast suitable for a Caribbean culinary connoisseur.

But Caymanian cuisine is not simply about fish and spices. The islands provide an assortment of fresh tropical fruits and vegetables that give a bright touch to every meal.

Enjoy luscious mangoes, sweet papayas, cool coconut water, and the island's namesake fruit, the pleasantly sour and acidic sorrel.

To satiate your sweet craving, make sure to indulge in local delicacies like coconut tart, heavy cake, and the famed Caymanian rum cake. These delicacies are rich in taste and give a lovely conclusion to any gastronomic adventure.

Here are 10 Caymanian cuisines you must try:

1. Cayman-style Turtle Stew: A favorite traditional meal, this stew comprises soft turtle flesh cooked with a combination of herbs, spices, and fresh vegetables. It is a substantial and savory dish that pays respect to the Cayman Islands' culinary history.

2. Jerk Chicken: Marinated in a fiery combination of Caribbean spices, jerk chicken is a succulent and spicy pleasure. The chicken is slow-cooked over open flames, resulting in soft flesh with a smokey and strong taste.

3. Caymanian Beef Patties: Similar to Jamaican beef patties, these delicious pastries are packed with seasoned ground beef covered in a flaky pastry casing. They make for a tasty on-the-go snack or a substantial supper.

4. Conch Fritters: Made with tender conch flesh blended with a savory batter, these deep-fried delicacies are crunchy on the exterior and soft on the inside. Served with a tangy dipping sauce, they are a favorite appetizer in the Cayman Islands.

5. Cayman-style BBQ Ribs: Slow-cooked to perfection, these delicious ribs are basted in a tangy and sweet barbecue sauce. The flesh is fall-off-the-bone delicious, making it a favorite among meat enthusiasts.

6. Heavy Cake: A thick and dense cake prepared with native ingredients such as cassava, coconut, and spices, a heavy cake is a classic Caymanian treat. It gives a lovely blend of sweetness and earthy tastes.

7. Caymanian Style Beef: This recipe comprises tender beef cooked with onions, peppers, and fragrant spices. The slow-cooked beef becomes soft and aromatic, culminating in a delightful main dish.

8. Cassava Cake: Made with grated cassava, coconut milk, and spices, this moist and sweet cake is a favorite dish in the Cayman Islands. It has a distinct texture and a lovely tropical taste.

9. Caymanian Style Chicken: A tasty chicken meal seasoned with a combination of indigenous spices and herbs, Caymanian-style chicken is often oven-roasted or grilled to perfection. It works nicely with traditional side dishes like rice and beans.

10. Johnny Cake: These golden, fluffy, and slightly sweet cornmeal cakes are a mainstay of Caymanian cuisine. They are commonly appreciated as a morning treat or as a side dish with savory dishes.

These Caymanian cuisine specialties give a sample of the islands' distinct tastes and culinary traditions, exhibiting the depth and complexity of the native food culture. Whether you're having a relaxed lunch with your toes in the sand, eating at an upscale waterfront restaurant, or experiencing street food at a local market, Caymanian cuisine promises to be a feast for your senses.

Vegetarian and Vegan Options

1. Plantain Fritters: Made from ripe plantains mashed and blended with flour and seasonings, these fritters are deep-fried to perfection.

They are crispy on the exterior and soft on the inside, making them a delightful vegetarian snack.

2. Callaloo: A classic Caribbean cuisine, callaloo is a savory stew cooked with leafy greens such as taro leaves or spinach. It is cooked with onions, garlic, tomatoes, and a variety of spices, resulting in a healthy and fulfilling vegetarian dinner.

3. Ackee and Vegetable Stir-Fry: Ackee, the national fruit of Jamaica, is sautéed with a mix of colorful vegetables including bell peppers, onions, and carrots. This savory and lively stir-fry is a fantastic vegetarian choice packed with Caribbean spices.

4. Plantain and Black Bean Tacos: Instead of usual meat fillings, these tacos utilize ripe plantains and seasoned black beans as the lead components. Served with fresh salsa, avocado, and a dash of lime, they create a lovely and hearty vegan lunch.

5. Coconut Curry with Vegetables: A fragrant and creamy curry created with a foundation of coconut milk, this meal is laden with a variety of vegetables such as bell peppers, carrots, cauliflower, and zucchini. It's a vegan-friendly choice that is both soothing and full of flavor.

6. Ackee with Plantain: A classic Caribbean meal, ackee is a fruit that mimics scrambled eggs when cooked. It is commonly coupled with sautéed ripe plantains, producing a wonderful and substantial vegetarian meal.

7. Vegetable Roti: Roti is a Caribbean flatbread, and when filled with a variety of sautéed veggies, it offers a filling and savory vegetarian choice. The blend of spices and textures makes it a popular option among vegetarians.

8. Rundown: This traditional meal is produced by cooking vegetables including pumpkin, sweet potato, and okra in a coconut milk base. It is a soothing and creamy meal that is appropriate for vegetarians as well.

9. Mango Salsa: With an abundance of tropical fruits in the Cayman Islands, a fresh and zesty mango salsa provides a pleasant vegetarian and vegan choice. Made with ripe mangoes, peppers, onions, and lime juice, it delivers a blast of flavors to any meal.

These vegetarian and vegan choices exhibit the ingenuity and variety of plant-based dishes in Caymanian cuisine, giving tasty alternatives for those seeking meat-free meals while discovering the colorful tastes of the islands.

Seafood Specialties

1. Cayman-style Fish Tacos: Made with fresh, flaky fish such as snapper or mahi-mahi, Cayman-style fish tacos are a popular seafood delicacy. The fish is seasoned with a combination of spices, grilled or fried to perfection, and served in a soft tortilla with tangy slaw and a spicy sauce.

2. Coconut Shrimp: Succulent shrimp wrapped in a crispy batter laced with shredded coconut is a wonderful seafood specialty in the Cayman Islands. Served with a sweet and tangy dipping sauce, coconut shrimp delivers a great blend of tastes and textures.

3. Grilled Lobster: With an abundance of fresh lobster in the nearby seas, grilled lobster is a must-try seafood dish. The sensitive lobster tail is marinated in a fragrant combination of herbs and spices, then grilled to perfection, resulting in a scrumptious meal that accentuates the inherent sweetness of the lobster flesh.

4. Caymanian-style Fish Escovitch: This meal mixes gently fried fish, generally snapper, with a sour and spicy sauce prepared from vinegar, onions, peppers, and spices. It is often served with rice and veggies.

5. Grilled Octopus: Tender and grilled octopus, marinated in a combination of herbs, spices, and citrus, is a seafood delicacy in the Cayman Islands. The smokey tastes and soft texture make it a favorite among seafood fans.

These seafood delicacies demonstrate the quantity of fresh and delectable seafood found in the Cayman Islands, enabling tourists to revel in the rich coastal tastes and discover the genuine spirit of the local cuisine.

Fine Dining and Gourmet Experiences

1. Grand Cayman - Blue by Eric Ripert

Blue by Eric Ripert is the lone restaurant in Grand Cayman that has been granted the coveted AAA Five Diamond rating. It proudly shows the freshest seafood taken from local waterways. Guests at Blue may indulge in expertly created prix fixe and tasting menus, enabling them to taste a varied spectrum of flavors and culinary wonders. The restaurant also features an amazing range of over 700 premium wines, complimenting the unique artisan cocktails that are masterfully created.

Location: The Ritz-Carlton, Seven Mile Beach, Grand Cayman

Close by landmarks: The Ritz-Carlton is a renowned luxury resort located on the famed Seven Mile Beach.

Opening and closing hours: Dinner service from 6:00 PM to 10:00 PM from Tuesday through Saturday, closed on Sundays and Mondays.

Accessibility: The restaurant is accessible with parking facilities provided.

Wheelchair access: Wheelchair access is provided.
View: The restaurant provides amazing views of the Caribbean Sea.

Setting and sitting position: The dining space is attractively arranged, with both indoor and outdoor seating choices available.

Services: Blue by Eric Ripert gives great service with attentive employees and a competent sommelier.

Price range: The price range is high-end, reflecting the gourmet experience and excellent ingredients.

Staff attitude: The staff is competent, pleasant, and knowledgeable about the cuisine.

Rating: I would grade it as a top-notch fine dining experience. The food is usually fresh and beautifully presented.

Dressing requirements: Smart casual wear is encouraged.

Kids and pets allowed: The restaurant is mainly suitable for adults and does not expressly cater to youngsters or allow pets.

Visitors' norms and etiquettes: Guests are required to maintain a courteous and classy environment.
Reservations: Reservations are strongly suggested and may be booked online or via their contact details below:

Website:
www.blue.ky
Phone:
+1 (345) 943-9000

2. Cayman Brac - Le Soleil d'Or Restaurant

Le Soleil d'Or restaurant stands out as the lone beachside farm-to-table experience in the Cayman Islands. Situated on the unspoiled Cayman Brac, a simple one-hour flight from Miami, tourists luxuriate in the opulent but casual ambiance of beach villas that provide special facilities including private pools and direct access to the beautiful beach.

Location: South Side Road, Stake Bay, Cayman Brac

Close by landmarks: The restaurant is located inside the Le Soleil d'Or Resort, surrounded by lovely gardens and overlooking the Caribbean Sea.

Opening and closing hours: Breakfast service from 8:00 AM to 10:30 AM, lunch service from 12:00 PM to 2:00 PM, and dinner service from 6:00 PM to 9:00 PM.

Accessibility: The restaurant is readily accessible by road.

Wheelchair access: Wheelchair access is provided.

View: The restaurant provides stunning views of the resort's gardens and the turquoise seas of the Caribbean.

Setting & seating position: The restaurant has a wonderful interior dining space and a lovely outside patio.

Services: Le Soleil d'Or Restaurant delivers personalized service with an emphasis on farm-to-table cuisine utilizing products derived from their organic farm.

Price range: The price range is upmarket, reflecting the gourmet farm-to-table experience.

Staff attitude: The staff is pleasant, welcoming, and knowledgeable about the cuisine.

Rating: I would rank it as an outstanding eating experience in Cayman Brac. It has a warm atmosphere and nice meals.

Dressing requirements: Smart casual wear is encouraged.
Kids and pets allowed: Children are welcome, while pets are not allowed.

Visitors' norms & etiquettes: Guests are encouraged to maintain a courteous and easygoing environment.
Reservations: Reservations are recommended and may be arranged by calling the restaurant directly:

Phone:
+1 (345) 769-8755

3. Little Cayman - Pirates Point Resort Dining Room
At Pirates Point, their cooking philosophy is simple as everything is created from scratch utilizing fresh ingredients. They avoid manufactured meals and respond to dietary restrictions and particular demands.

Incorporating local delicacies like lionfish, mangos, and tomatoes, their menus contain a variety of meals from classics to contemporary innovations. Friday evenings provide a unique treat with a hand-made Sushi happy hour followed by a full meal and delectable desserts. Reservations must be made before noon on the dinner day to accommodate additional guests. With a fully stocked bar and snacks offered before dinner, Pirates Point offers a memorable and delightful dining experience.

Location: Pirates Point Road, Blossom Village, Little Cayman

Close by landmarks: The dining room is part of the Pirates Point Resort, situated in the center of Blossom Village.

Opening and closing hours: Breakfast service from 7:30 AM to 9:00 AM, lunch service from 12:30 PM to 2:00 PM, and dinner service from 6:30 PM to 8:00 PM.

Accessibility: The resort is readily accessible by car.

Wheelchair access: Wheelchair access is provided.

View: The dining area overlooks the resort's tropical gardens and the crystal-clear seas of Little Cayman.

Setting and sitting position: The dining area provides a warm and intimate ambiance with comfortable seating options.

Services: The Pirates Point Resort Dining Room delivers personalized service and specializes in gourmet Caribbean cuisine with an emphasis on locally produced ingredients.

Price range: The price range is greater owing to the gourmet dining experience and individual attention.

Staff attitude: The staff is polite, helpful, and dedicated to creating a wonderful dining experience.

Rating: I would describe it as a unique and enjoyable dining experience in Little Cayman.

Dressing requirements: Smart casual wear is encouraged.
Kids and pets permitted: Children are welcome, while pets are not allowed.

Visitors' norms & etiquettes: Guests are urged to respect the calm island environment and appreciate the tranquility of the surroundings.

Reservations: Reservations are necessary and may be arranged by calling the resort directly:

Website:
www.piratespointresort.com
Phone:
+1 (345) 948-1010

Local Restaurants and Street Food

1. Grand Cayman: The Brasserie

The Brasserie is a famous farm-to-table restaurant situated in George Town, Grand Cayman. It provides a distinct culinary experience with an emphasis on fresh, locally produced foods.

Location: Cricket Square, 171 Elgin Avenue, George Town, Grand Cayman.

Close by landmarks: Cricket Square is a notable commercial complex in George Town.

Opening and Closing Hours: Monday to Friday from 11:30 AM to 2:30 PM for lunch, and Monday to Saturday from 5:30 PM for supper.

Accessibility: The Brasserie is readily accessible by road in downtown George Town.

Wheelchair Access: Wheelchair access is provided.
View: The restaurant boasts a wonderful garden setting with rich foliage.

Setting & Sitting Position: The Brasserie provides indoor and outdoor dining choices in a comfortable and classy ambiance.
Services: The Brasserie delivers attentive service with a skilled staff.

Price Range: The price range is moderate to high, indicating the quality of ingredients and eating experience.

Staff Attitude: The staff is pleasant, professional, and enthusiastic about the farm-to-table idea.

Rating: I would rank it as an amazing dining experience in Grand Cayman.

Dressing Requirements: Smart casual wear is preferred.

Kids and Pets allowed: Children are welcome, and pets are not permitted.

Visitors Rules & Etiquettes: Guests are encouraged to respect the luxury eating ambiance and enjoy the farm-fresh food.

Reservations: Reservations may be arranged by calling The Brasserie

Website:
www.brasseriecayman.com
Phone:
+1 (345) 945-1815

2. Cayman Brac: Star Island Restaurant
Star Island Restaurant is a quaint small cafe on Cayman Brac, giving a taste of classic Caymanian food with a comfortable island feel.

Location: Stake Bay Road, Cayman Brac.

Landmarks: The restaurant is located in the center of Stake Bay, the major town of Cayman Brac.

Opening and Closing Hours: Monday to Saturday from 11:00 AM to 8:00 PM.

Accessibility: The restaurant is readily accessible by road in Stake Bay.

Wheelchair Access: Wheelchair access is provided.

View: The restaurant provides vistas of the Caribbean Sea and neighboring shorelines.

Setting & Sitting Position: Star Island Restaurant has indoor and outdoor sitting choices, including patio seating.

Services: The restaurant offers courteous and attentive service, delivering a sample of local food.

Price Range: The price range is reasonable, reflecting the informal eating experience.

Staff Attitude: The staff is pleasant and knowledgeable about Caymanian food.

Rating: I would describe it as a lovely venue to experience native delicacies on Cayman Brac.

Dressing Requirements: Casual clothes are appropriate.

Kids and Pets allowed: Children are welcome, and pets may not be permitted.

Visitors Rules & Etiquettes: Guests are urged to appreciate the laid-back island ambiance and enjoy the native food.

Reservations: Reservations may be obtained by calling Star Island Restaurant

Phone:
+1 (345) 948-2100

3. Little Cayman: Hungry Iguana

The Hungry Iguana is a famous beachside restaurant and bar in Little Cayman, providing a casual and tropical eating experience.

Location: Blossom Village, Little Cayman.

Landmarks: The restaurant is situated in the middle of Blossom Village, the major village in Little Cayman.

Opening and Closing Hours: Monday to Sunday from 11:00 AM to 10:00 PM.

Accessibility: The eatery is readily accessible in Blossom Village.

Wheelchair Access: Wheelchair access may be restricted owing to the beachside setting.

View: The restaurant boasts breathtaking views of the Caribbean Sea and sandy beaches.

Setting & Sitting Position: The Hungry Iguana provides both indoor and outdoor sitting choices, including beachside tables.

Services: The restaurant provides pleasant service with a beachy feel, delivering a range of cuisine and refreshing beverages.

Price Range: The price range is reasonable, and perfect for casual seaside eating.

Staff Attitude: The staff is laid-back and accommodating, reflecting the island lifestyle.

Rating: I would rank it as a terrific site to have lunch while soaking in the beach vibe in Little Cayman.

Dressing Requirements: Casual beachwear is acceptable.
Kids and Pets allowed: Children are welcome, and pets may not be permitted.

Visitors Rules & Etiquettes: Guests are urged to relax, appreciate the seaside location, and experience the flavors of the Caribbean.

Reservations: Reservations may be arranged by calling the Hungry Iguana:

Phone:
+1 (345) 948-0003

Beach Bars and Nightlife Hotspots

1. Grand Cayman

Beach Bar: Tiki Beach
Tiki Beach is a bustling beach bar situated on the gorgeous Seven Mile Beach. It provides a tropical environment, live music, and a choice of refreshing beverages and cocktails.

Location: West Bay Road, Seven Mile Beach, Grand Cayman.

Landmarks: Tiki Beach is located along Seven Mile Beach, near Camana Bay.

Opening and Closing Hours: Daily from 11:00 AM to late at night.

Accessibility: Tiki Beach is readily accessible along West Bay Road, with parking provided nearby.

Wheelchair Access: Wheelchair access is provided, with ramps and accessible amenities.

View: The bar boasts stunning views of Seven Mile Beach and the crystal-clear seas of the Caribbean Sea.

Setting & Sitting Position: Tiki Beach provides both beachside sitting and a bustling bar area, with lounge chairs and umbrellas accessible for visitors.

Services: The bar provides a large assortment of tropical drinks, beers, and spirits, along with a menu of appetizers and seaside snacks.

Price Range: The pricing range is reasonable, reflecting the beachside setting and energetic environment.

Staff Attitude: The staff is courteous, and enthusiastic, and delivers outstanding service.

Rating: Tiki Beach is ranked as a top beach bar hotspot with its energetic atmosphere and magnificent beach views.

Positive Aspects: Beautiful seaside setting, live music, vibrant vibe.

Negative Aspects: Potential crowds at peak hours.

Dressing Requirements: Casual beachwear is appropriate.

Kids and pets permitted: Children and dogs are permitted in certain places.

Visitors Rules and Etiquettes: Guests are encouraged to enjoy themselves responsibly and respect the beach environment.

Reservations: Reservations are requested for bigger parties and special events.Contact Info:

Phone:
+1 (345) 945-3800
Website:
www.tikibeachcayman.com

Nightlife Hotspot: O Bar
O Bar is a popular nightlife destination situated in Queens Court Plaza. It provides a trendy environment, distinctive drinks, and a dynamic atmosphere for partygoers.

Location: Queens Court Plaza, Seven Mile Beach, Grand Cayman.

Landmarks: O Bar is located in Queens Court Plaza, among numerous other renowned bars and restaurants.

Opening and Closing Hours: Daily from 6:00 PM to late at night.

Accessibility: O Bar is readily accessible, with parking provided nearby.

Wheelchair Access: Wheelchair access is offered by elevators and ramps.

View: The pub provides a trendy and contemporary environment, but no distinctive view.

Setting & Sitting Position: O Bar boasts a modern interior design with comfortable sitting choices, including lounge spaces and high-top tables.

Services: The bar focuses on artisan cocktails, premium spirits, and a range of wines and beers.

Price Range: The price range is moderate to upmarket, reflecting the fashionable ambiance and excellent drinks.

Staff Attitude: The staff is professional, knowledgeable, and delivers attentive service.

Rating: O Bar is considered a top nightlife location, giving a refined and lively experience.

Positive Aspects: Stylish ambiance, specialty drinks, energetic vibe.

Negative Aspects: Potential crowds at peak hours, limited space.

Dressing Requirements: Smart-casual attire is encouraged.

Kids and Pets Allowed: O Bar is an adult-oriented establishment and may not admit kids or dogs.

Visitors Rules & Etiquettes: Guests are required to maintain a polite and courteous demeanor.

Reservations: Reservations are suggested, particularly on weekends or for special events.
Contact Info:

Phone:
+1 (345) 943-6227
Website:
www.obargc.com

2. Cayman Brac

Beach Bar: The Captain's Table

The Captain's Table is a lovely beach bar tucked on the south side of Cayman Brac. It provides a laid-back environment, amazing ocean views, and a menu of tropical cocktails.

Location: South Side Road, Cayman Brac, Cayman Islands.

Landmarks: The Captain's Table is situated between the Brac Reef Beach Resort and the Bluff View Art District.

Opening and Closing Hours: Daily from 11:00 AM to 10:00 PM.

Accessibility: The beach bar is readily accessible by cars, with parking available nearby.

Wheelchair Access: The business is wheelchair accessible, with ramps and accessible amenities.

View: The Captain's Table affords panoramic views of the Caribbean Sea and the picturesque shoreline of Cayman Brac.

Setting & Sitting Position: The beach bar provides both indoor and outdoor sitting choices, enabling customers to enjoy their beverages with the sand under their toes or at nice tables inside.

Services: The bar provides a range of refreshing drinks, including local delicacies, as well as a selection of beers and non-alcoholic beverages.

Price Range: The costs are low, making it a popular option among residents and tourists.

Staff Attitude: The staff is courteous, inviting, and delivers attentive service.

Rating: The Captain's Table is recognized as a beautiful beach bar with spectacular views and an easygoing environment.

Positive Aspects: Scenic setting, helpful personnel, cheap costs.
Negative Aspects: Limited food menu.

Dressing Requirements: Casual beachwear is appropriate.
Kids and Pets Allowed: Children and dogs are welcome in the outside dining area.

Visitors Rules & Etiquettes: Guests are asked to maintain cleanliness and respect the natural environment.

Reservations: Reservations are not necessary but are encouraged for bigger parties.
Contact Info:

Phone:
+1 (345) 948-1333

Nightlife Hotspot: The Cayman Brac Sports Club & Restaurant
The Cayman Brac Sports Club & Restaurant is a busy nightlife destination that provides a blend of sports entertainment, live music, and a dynamic environment for residents and guests.

Location: 23 West End Road, West End, Cayman Brac, Cayman Islands.

Landmarks: The institution is located near the West End Public Beach and the Cayman Brac Heritage House.

Opening and Closing Hours: Monday to Saturday from 5:00 PM to 1:00 AM (closed on Sundays).

Accessibility: The Sports Club & Restaurant is readily accessible, with parking available nearby.

Wheelchair Access: The facility is wheelchair accessible, with ramps and accessible amenities.

View: While there may not be a particular view, the bustling atmosphere and entertainment make up for it.

Setting & Sitting Position: The restaurant has a huge inside space with a bar, dancing floor, and sitting choices, as well as an outside terrace for enjoying the Caribbean air.

Services: The Sports Club & Restaurant serves a variety of drinks, including a choice of beers, spirits, and cocktails. They also provide a range of appetizers and bar food.

Price Range: The costs are modest, catering to varied budgets.

Staff Attitude: The crew is lively, and responsive, and offers an enjoyable experience for all clients.

Rating: The Cayman Brac Sports Club & Restaurant is classified as a bustling nightlife center, excellent for mingling and enjoying entertainment.

Beach Bar: Hungry Iguana
Hungry Iguana has a laid-back and tropical environment, making it a popular hangout location for both residents and visitors.

Location: Blossom Village, Little Cayman, Cayman Islands.

Landmarks: The beach bar is located near the Little Cayman Museum and the Salt Rock Nature Trail.

Opening and Closing Hours: Daily from 11:00 AM to 10:00 PM.

Accessibility: The Hungry Iguana is readily accessible inside Blossom Village, with close parking available.

Wheelchair Access: The business is wheelchair accessible, with ramps and accessible amenities.

View: The beach bar affords spectacular views of the blue Caribbean Sea and the clean sandy beach.

Setting & Sitting Position: Guests may opt to relax at outside tables with beachside views or have a drink at the busy bar.

Services: Hungry Iguana provides a selection of tropical drinks, local beers, and non-alcoholic beverages. They also provide a menu offering delectable Caribbean-inspired cuisine and bar snacks.

Price Range: The prices are moderate, delivering value for money.

Staff Attitude: The staff is pleasant, and attentive, and provides a welcoming environment for customers.

Rating: Hungry Iguana is ranked as a top beach bar, providing a lovely combination of spectacular vistas, pleasant beverages, and excellent cuisine.

Positive Aspects: Scenic seaside setting, courteous service, a wonderful meal, and beverages.

Negative Aspects: Limited seats during peak hours.

Dressing Requirements: Casual beach wear is appropriate.

Kids and Pets Allowed: Children and well-behaved dogs are allowed in the outside sitting area.

Visitors Rules and Etiquettes: Guests are asked to respect the beach and clean up after themselves.

Reservations: Reservations are not necessary for individuals or small parties.
Contact Info:

Phone:
+1 (345) 948-0000

3. Little Cayman

Nightlife Hotspot: The Southern Cross Club
The Southern Cross Club provides a stylish and comfortable ambiance, giving visitors a wonderful evening experience.

Location: South Hole Sound, Little Cayman, Cayman Islands.

Landmarks: The Southern Cross Club is located near Owen Island and the famed Bloody Bay Wall diving location.

Opening and Closing Hours: Varies based on events and activities. Contact the resort for the latest information.

Accessibility: The resort is readily accessible by car or boat, with transportation choices available on the island.

Wheelchair Access: The facility is wheelchair accessible, with ramps and accessible amenities.

View: The Southern Cross Club provides wonderful views of the Caribbean Sea and the surrounding natural beauty of Little Cayman.

Setting & Sitting Position: Guests may relax in the resort's lounge rooms, bar, or outside terrace, enjoying the quiet ambiance and interacting with other guests.

Services: The Southern Cross Club includes a well-stocked bar with a broad range of quality spirits, wines, and cocktails. They also give a choice of gourmet food alternatives.

Price Range: The costs are higher owing to the luxury character of the resort, delivering a pleasant experience.

Staff Attitude: The crew is professional, responsive, and attends to the demands of customers, creating a great night.
Rating: The Southern Cross Club is classified as an up-market nightlife.

SHOPPING
AND
SOUVENIRS

As you tour the lively and enchanting Cayman Islands, you'll uncover a treasure mine of shopping choices. From lively markets to elegant stores, this chapter is your tour of the eclectic retail environment that greets you. Whether you're seeking unique keepsakes to recall your vacation or want to indulge in some retail therapy, the Cayman Islands provide something for everyone.

Immerse yourself in the local culture as you browse around colorful markets, chat with friendly sellers, and unearth hidden jewels. From handcrafted crafts to high-end couture, the Cayman Islands offer a selection of shopping experiences that appeal to every taste and budget. Indulge in the island's particular charm as you examine local artwork, savor delectable delicacies, and locate that ideal keepsake to bring back home.

Join me as I take you on a trip around the busy shopping areas, highlight the must-visit businesses, and give insider secrets.
So, take your shopping bags and get ready to experience the lively world of shopping and souvenirs in this tropical paradise.

Duty-Free Shopping

1. Grand Cayman: Kirk Freeport
Kirk Freeport is a prominent duty-free shopping center in Grand Cayman. Located in the center of GeorgeTown, it provides a broad choice of luxury items like jewelry, watches, perfumes, accessories, and more. The store boasts a contemporary and attractive atmosphere, giving a premium shopping experience.

Location: Cardinal Avenue, George Town, Grand Cayman

Close by landmarks: George Town shoreline, Cayman Islands National Museum

Opening hours: Monday to Saturday from 9:00 AM to 5:00 PM

View: Enjoy views of the lively streets of George Town.

Services: Knowledgeable and cheerful personnel, tax-free shopping, gift wrapping services.

Price range: Mid to high-end, appealing to diverse budgets.

Staff attitude: Professional and attentive.

Rating: Highly rated for its vast range and good customer service.

Positive aspects: Wide choice of luxury items, accessible location, tax-free shopping.

Negative aspects: Prices may be higher compared to other destinations.

Dressing requirements: Smart-casual wear is suitable.

Kids and pets: Children are welcome, pets may not be permitted inside the shop.

Visitors' regulations and etiquette: Follow the store's requirements, and respect other consumers.

What to look out for: Check for any current specials or discounts.

Payment options: Credit cards, cash.

Bargaining: Typically not applicable in duty-free stores.

Safety: The business provides a safe and secure shopping environment.

2. Cayman Brac: Brac Scuba Shack

Brac Scuba Shack is a duty-free business situated in Cayman Brac, catering to scuba diving aficionados. It provides a large assortment of diving equipment, accessories, and clothes. The business is noted for its pleasant and experienced personnel, giving individual service to diving enthusiasts visiting the island.

Location: South Side Road, Cayman Brac

Close by landmarks: Cayman Brac Museum, Brac Reef Beach

Opening hours: Monday to Saturday from 8:00 AM to 5:00 PM

View: Enjoy views of the gorgeous Cayman Brac shoreline.

Services: Expert guidance, equipment rentals, and equipment maintenance.

Price range: Varies depending on the diving equipment and accessories.

Staff attitude: Friendly, knowledgeable, and helpful.

Rating: Highly regarded for their quality diving gear and good customer service.

Positive aspects: Extensive range of diving equipment, customized service.

Negative aspects: Limited non-diving related things offered. Dressing requirements: Casual attire.

Kids and pets: Children are welcome, pets may not be permitted inside the business.

Visitors' regulations and etiquette: Respect the store's norms and fellow divers.

What to look out for: Check for any special specials or bundle offers.

Payment options: Credit cards, cash.

Bargaining: Typically not applicable in duty-free stores.

Safety: The store provides a safe and well-equipped environment for divers.

3. Little Cayman: Little Cayman Beach Resort Gift Shop
The Little Cayman Beach Resort Gift Boutique is a duty-free boutique selling a selection of souvenirs, local crafts, clothes, and beach accessories. Located inside the Little Cayman Beach Resort, it offers guests and visitors a convenient shopping experience to locate unique keepsakes and beach supplies.

Location: Blossom Village, Little Cayman

Close by landmarks: Blossom Village Beach, Booby Pond Nature Reserve

Opening hours: Daily from 9:00 AM until 6:00 PM

View: Enjoy views of the lovely Caribbean Sea and a clean beach.

Services: Friendly personnel, gift wrapping services, local artisan items.

Price range: Varied, ideal for varied budgets.
Staff attitude: Welcoming and attentive.

Rating: Highly regarded for its collection of local items and polite service.

Positive aspects: Convenient location, varied souvenir selections.

Negative aspects: Limited variety compared to bigger retailers.

Dressing requirements: Casual attire.

Kids and pets: Children are welcome, pets may not be permitted inside the business.

Visitors' norms and etiquette: Respect the resort's requirements and fellow visitors.

What to look out for: Look for any distinctive local crafts or homemade items.

Payment options: Credit cards, cash.

Bargaining: Typically not relevant for souvenir businesses.

Safety: The store operates inside the guarded resort grounds.

Local Art and Craft Markets

1. Grand Cayman - Camana Bay Artisan Market
Nestled in the bustling village of Camana Bay, the Artisan Market highlights the abilities of local artists and craftspeople. Explore a broad assortment of handcrafted jewelry, paintings, ceramics, and other unique crafts.

Location: Camana Bay, Grand Cayman

Close by Landmarks: Camana Bay Town Centre, Seven Mile Beach

Opening and Closing Hours: Saturdays from 10:00 AM until 3:00 PM

View: Enjoy a lovely location with nicely planted surrounds and a delightful waterfront vibe.

Services: Friendly merchants share insights into their crafts and provide individual advice.

Price Range: Varied, ideal for varied budgets.

Staff Attitude: Welcoming and passionate, willing to reveal the story behind their products.

Rating: Highly regarded for its great assortment of local art and crafts.

Positive Aspects: A terrific chance to support local craftspeople, discover unique gifts, and participate in cultural interaction.

Negative Aspects: Limited working hours may demand preparation in advance.

Dressing Requirements: Casual clothes are appropriate.

Kids and pets: Both kids and dogs are allowed to join you as you peruse the market.

Visitors Rules & Etiquettes: Respect the artists' work and ask for permission before taking images. Be respectful of other guests and keep a good environment.

What to Watch Out for: Some products may be fragile, so treat them with care.

Payment Options: Cash and credit/debit cards are often accepted.

Bargaining: Limited bargaining is generally conducted, particularly for bigger transactions.

Safety: The market is well-maintained and deemed safe for tourists.

2. Cayman Brac - Heritage House Craft Market
Situated in a lovely cottage-style structure, the legacy House Craft Market displays the rich legacy and creative traditions of Cayman Brac. Discover locally crafted crafts, woodwork, textiles, and more.

Location: West End Road, Cayman Brac

Close by Landmarks: Cayman Brac Museum, West End Point, Brac Reef Beach

Opening and Closing Hours: Monday to Friday from 9:00 AM to 4:00 PM

View: Surrounded by thick flora and wonderful sea vistas, providing a tranquil ambiance.

Services: Knowledgeable staff members give insights into the cultural importance of the crafts.

Price Range: Affordable, ideal for diverse budgets.

Staff Attitude: Friendly and dedicated to maintaining Cayman Brac's unique history.

Rating: Highly regarded for its genuine crafts and kind welcome.

Positive Aspects: Opportunities to support local craftspeople, learn about Cayman Brac's customs, and discover unique souvenirs.

Negative Aspects: Limited opening hours may need preparation.

Dressing Requirements: Casual clothes are appropriate.

Kids and Pets: Both kids and pets are welcome at the market.

Visitors Rules & Etiquettes: Respect the workmanship and cultural value of the artifacts. Handle sensitive goods with care and create a respectful attitude.

What to Watch Out for: Some goods may have particular care recommendations, so enquire before buying.

Payment Options: Cash is the preferred payment option, however, certain businesses may take credit/debit cards.

Bargaining: Limited bargaining may be feasible, particularly for bigger transactions.

Safety: The market is rated safe for tourists.

3. Little Cayman - Blossom Village Craft Market

The Blossom Village Craft Market displays the ingenuity and skill of local craftspeople in Little Cayman. Explore a selection of handcrafted jewelry, artwork, textiles, and other crafts.

Location: Blossom Village, Little Cayman

Close by Landmarks: Little Cayman Museum, Owen Island, Point of Sand

Opening and Closing Hours: Tuesday and Thursday from 9:00 AM to 12:00 PM

View: The market is situated in the middle of Blossom Village, affording vistas of the island's picturesque coastline backdrop.

Services: Friendly merchants share insights into their crafts and provide individual advice.

Price Range: Varies, catering to varied budgets.

Staff Attitude: Welcoming and passionate, keen to share their skill and local knowledge.

Rating: Highly acclaimed for its original local crafts and pleasant environment.

Positive Aspects: Support local craftspeople, find unique mementos, and participate with the community.

Negative Aspects: Limited operating hours may necessitate planning.

Dressing Requirements: Casual clothes are appropriate.

Kids and Pets: Both kids and pets are welcome at the market.

Visitors Rules & Etiquettes: Respect the artists' work and ask for permission before taking images. Treat the crafts with care and create a welcoming environment.

What to Watch Out for: Some crafts may be fragile, so treat them cautiously.

Payment Options: Cash is the preferred payment option, however, certain businesses may take credit/debit cards.

Negotiating: Limited negotiating possibilities may be available.

Safety: The market is rated safe for tourists.

Rare Souvenirs to Bring Home

1. Caymanite Jewelry: Caymanite is a rare semi-precious stone found uniquely in the Cayman Islands. Crafted into stunning jewelry items like pendants, earrings, and bracelets, Caymanite depicts the island's natural beauty. Prices might vary based on the size and complexity of the artwork. Payment may be paid in cash or with credit/debit cards at local jewelry shops or artisan markets.

2. Tortuga Rum Cake: This delightful dessert is a must-try memento. Made with local rum and a secret recipe, Tortuga Rum Cake reflects the tastes of the Caribbean. It comes in several sizes and flavors including original, chocolate, and key lime. Prices vary from roughly USD 10 to $25 depending on the size. Payment may be done in cash or with credit/debit cards at gift stores or supermarkets.

3. Black Coral Jewelry: Black coral is a rare and protected species found in the seas around the Cayman Islands. Local artists produce gorgeous jewelry items, such as necklaces, earrings, and rings, from sustainably harvested black coral. These unique items highlight the beauty and protection of Cayman's aquatic environment. Prices might vary based on the design and size. Payment is often done in cash or using credit/debit cards at approved shops.

4. Cayman Sea Salt: Produced from crystal-clear waters around the islands, Cayman sea salt has a tasty and distinctive taste. Packaged in attractive containers, it makes for a handy and genuine keepsake. Prices normally vary from $5 to $15 depending on the size. Payment is mainly done in cash or with credit/debit cards at specialist stores or souvenir shops. Cash or card payments are allowed.

5. Camana Bay Sand Jewelry: Handcrafted with sand obtained from the famed Seven Mile Beach, Camana Bay sand jewelry reflects the spirit of the Cayman Islands' magnificent shoreline. These distinctive items, such as necklaces and bracelets, serve as wearable mementos of the island's gorgeous beaches. Prices vary from roughly $15 to $40 depending on the design.

6. Cayman Islands Artisanal Rum: The Cayman Islands manufacture their unique artisanal rums, frequently flavored with native tastes like coconut, mango, or spices. These rums showcase the islands' rich rum-making traditions and make for a wonderful and genuine keepsake. Prices vary based on the brand and size. Payment may be done in cash or with credit/debit cards at liquor stores or duty-free shops.

7. Conch Shell Crafts: Conch shells are a symbol of the Caribbean and are made into unique crafts including jewelry, decorations, and ornamental objects. These shells signify the islands' marine life and seaside attractiveness. Prices vary based on the size and intricacy of the craft. Payment is frequently paid in cash at local artisan markets or specialized businesses.

Snorkling

Scuba Diving

OUTDOOR
ADVENTURES
AND
WATERSPORTS

CHAPTER EIGHT

Welcome to Chapter 8 of our guide, where we dive into the amazing world of outdoor activities and water-sports in the Cayman Islands.

Embark on an extraordinary trip as we explore the exhilarating water-based activities, adrenaline-pumping excursions, and mesmerizing natural treasures that await you in the Cayman Islands. Whether you are seeking undersea exploration, heart-racing water activities, or magnificent excursions through the undisturbed wilderness, this chapter will be your thorough guide to enjoying the finest of the great outdoors in the Cayman Islands.

So, gather your gear, get ready to make a splash, and let's plunge into the exhilarating world of outdoor activities and watersports in the intriguing Cayman Islands.

Scuba Diving and Snorkeling

The Cayman Islands are famous for their fantastic scuba diving and snorkeling possibilities. With crystal-clear seas and vivid coral reefs, it's a paradise for underwater exploration. Here are some great sites for first-time scuba divers and snorkelers on each of the islands:

Grand Cayman: One of the most popular diving locations is the famed Stingray City, where you may swim with gentle stingrays in shallow seas. For scuba diving, the Kittiwake Shipwreck and the North Wall provide beautiful underwater scenery and varied marine life.

Cayman Brac: Explore the MV Captain Keith Tibbetts wreck, a sunken Russian ship that today functions as an artificial reef. The Buccaneer Reef and Radar Reef are both wonderful snorkeling places with beautiful corals and exotic fish.

Little Cayman: Bloody Bay Marine Park is a must-visit for both snorkelers and scuba divers. The immaculate coral gardens and rich aquatic life will leave you in amazement. The Mixing Bowl and Jackson's Bight are both popular places for underwater aficionados.

Safety Tips
1. Always dive or snorkel with a companion and follow the recommendations of certified experts.
2. Check your equipment before each dive or snorkel session and verify it is in excellent operating order.
3. Familiarize yourself with local diving and snorkeling rules and abide by them.
4. Respect the aquatic environment and avoid harming or injuring coral and marine life.
5. Watch instructions for boat traffic and remain inside permitted swimming zones.
6. Stay hydrated and protect yourself from the sun by wearing sunscreen and a hat.
7. Be cautious of your boundaries and don't push yourself beyond your comfort zone.

Sailing and Boating

The Cayman Islands provide a fantastic sailing and boating experience, with its quiet and crystal-clear seas. Whether you're a seasoned sailor or a first-time boater, there are plenty of possibilities to explore.

Grand Cayman is home to various marinas and yacht clubs, such as Camana Bay and The Yacht Club, providing boat rentals and charters. Sail along the shoreline, explore adjacent Stingray City or cruise to scenic Seven Mile Beach.

In **Cayman Brac**, travel to Creek Dock or Stake Bay Dock for boat rentals and guided tours.

Explore the island's magnificent shoreline, see the famed Cayman Brac Lighthouse, or find secret coves and isolated beaches.

Little Cayman also provides sailing and boating options, with Point of Sand and South Hole Sound being popular places. Rent a boat and sail the tranquil waters, enjoy fishing, or just relax and take in the island's natural beauty.

Safety Tips
1. Always use a personal flotation device (PFD) or life jacket.
2. Start in calm and shallow waters to feel comfortable before exploring deeper.
3. Be mindful of weather conditions and tides before venturing out.
4. Stay hydrated and wear sunscreen to defend against the sun's rays.
5. Respect marine life and coral reefs by avoiding touch and maintaining a safe distance.

Kayaking and Paddle-boarding

Kayaking and Paddle-boarding in the Cayman Islands provide a terrific opportunity to explore the clean seas and picturesque coasts. For first-time explorers, here are some suggested spots on each island to undertake these activities:

Grand Cayman: The tranquil waters of Seven Mile Beach and Rum Point are great for kayaking and paddleboarding. Beginners may enjoy the peaceful bays and clean seas while enjoying the picturesque surroundings.

Cayman Brac: Head to the South Side of the island for kayaking and paddleboarding in the remote and tranquil seas. The reef-protected sections offer a secure and tranquil experience for novices.

Little Cayman: Owen Island and Point of Sand Beach are good sites for kayaking and paddleboarding. The tranquil lagoons and shallow reefs make it simple for first-timers to explore and appreciate the beauty of the island.

Fishing Excursions

Fishing Excursions in the Cayman Islands provide an exciting experience for both seasoned anglers and first-time fishers. Each island offers distinct fishing places that appeal to various interests and ability levels.

Grand Cayman: Head to the North Sound or South Sound for a range of fishing choices. The North Sound provides deep-sea fishing cruises targeting marlin, tuna, and mahi-mahi. on the South Sound, you may try bonefishing on the shallow flats, suitable for novices.

Cayman Brac: This island is recognized for its superb reef fishing. Explore areas like Spot Bay, Jackson's Bight, or the Brac Reef for a chance to capture snapper, grouper, and other colorful reef species.

Little Cayman: Venture to Owen Island or the Bloody Bay Wall for spectacular offshore fishing. Test your abilities against wahoo, barracuda, and even the elusive sailfish.

Safety Tips
1. Ensure you have a valid fishing license, which can be purchased through the Cayman Islands Department of Environment.
2. Follow catch limits and size standards to safeguard the marine habitat.
3. Be careful of weather conditions and always wear adequate safety gear.
4. If unfamiliar with the waterways, consider hiring a local fishing guide for extra safety and assistance.

Eco-Tours and Nature Walks

Eco-Tours & Nature Walks in the Cayman Islands give you the ideal chance to immerse yourself in the natural splendor of these lovely islands. Here are some excellent sites for first-timers to explore:

Grand Cayman: Queen Elizabeth II Botanic Park - This enormous park includes various flora and fauna, walking pathways, and guided tours, enabling visitors to experience the island's unique plants and animals.

Cayman Brac: The Brac Parrot Reserve - A refuge for bird watchers, this area is home to the endangered Cayman Brac Parrot. Visitors may go on guided nature excursions to witness these amazing birds in their native environment.

Little Cayman: Booby Pond Nature Reserve - This reserve is a refuge for the red-footed booby, a local seabird species. Guided excursions take tourists into the reserve's wetlands, where they may watch nesting colonies and learn about the island's biodiversity.

Safety Tips
1. Stay on authorized routes and trails to conserve sensitive habitats.
2. Respect animals by viewing them from a distance and abstaining from feeding or touching them.
3. Pack necessities such as sunscreen, bug protection, and drinking water.
4. Observe any posted signs or rules regarding protected places and limited activities.
5. Follow all local rules and regulations, including getting any licenses for fishing, camping, or other outdoor activities.

Caving and Exploration

The Cayman Islands provide unique chances for caving and exploration, enabling tourists to uncover hidden delights under the surface. Here are some areas where first-timers may go on cave-exploring adventures:

Grand Cayman: The Mastic Reserve and Cayman Crystal Caves are two popular places for caving. Explore the intriguing limestone formations, stalactites, and stalagmites in these well-preserved caverns.

Cayman Brac: The Bat Cave and Peter's Cave are must-visit places for caving aficionados. Marvel at the natural beauty and fascinating rock formations as you delve into the depths of these mesmerizing caverns.

Little Cayman: Owen's Island Cave and The Great Cave are famous destinations for cave exploring. Discover the subterranean treasures and immerse yourself in the rich history of these ancient caverns.

Safety Tips
1. Always visit caves with an expert guide or tour operator who can give information and assure your safety.
2. Wear suitable gear and footwear for cave exploration, including a helmet and strong shoes with excellent grip.
3. Carry required tools such as a flashlight, additional batteries, and a first aid kit.
4. Respect the environment and leave no trace behind.
5. Avoid harming or eliminating any structures or creatures.
6. Follow any norms and regulations issued by the government or tour companies regulating cave exploring.
7. Remember, cave exploring may be physically hard and sometimes dangerous. It is crucial to prioritize your safety and comply with all safety standards to make the most of your caving adventure in the Cayman Islands.

Cycling and Hiking Trails

1. Grand Cayman

Mastic track: Explore the pristine environment of the Mastic Reserve on this picturesque hiking track. It provides a broad mix of flora and wildlife, with choices for both novices and expert hikers. Remember to wear suitable hiking shoes, bring adequate water, and be cautious of the trail's rough terrain.

East-West Arterial Bikeway: Perfect for cycling enthusiasts, this dedicated bike lane runs along the East-West Arterial road. Enjoy a comfortable ride while taking in the gorgeous coastline sights. Remember to wear a helmet, respect traffic regulations, and be aware of other road users.

2. Cayman Brac

Brac Parrot Reserve track: Immerse yourself in the luxuriant foliage of the Brac Parrot Reserve on this gorgeous hiking track. Observe the natural fauna and enjoy panoramic views of the island. Wear sturdy shoes, carry bug repellent, and be cautious of possibly steep areas.

Southside Loop: Cyclists may enjoy the lovely Southside Loop, a path that encircles the southern section of the island. Take in the gorgeous coastline landscape while complying with traffic safety requirements, such as utilizing hand signals and cycling in a single file.

3. Little Cayman

Booby Pond Nature Reserve Trail: Explore the intriguing Booby Pond Nature Reserve by foot, home to a broad assortment of bird species. Follow the specified routes and respect the delicate habitat.

Wear sunscreen, bring binoculars, and stay a safe distance from animals.

Blossom Village Loop: Cycle around Blossom Village, the major village on Little Cayman. Enjoy the laid-back vibe as you cycle around peaceful roads. Stay visible with luminous clothes, utilize hand signals, and be conscious of local traffic restrictions.

Safety Tips

1. Always pack adequate water, food, and sun protection while outdoor activities.

2. Stick to authorized trails and walkways to maintain the natural environment.

3. Wear suitable footwear and gear for comfort and protection.

4. Follow traffic regulations and be careful of other road users while riding.

5. Respect animals and their habitats, maintaining a safe distance.

6. Inform someone of your goals and approximate return time before hiking or riding alone.

7. Stay hydrated, pace yourself, and be prepared for changing weather conditions.

Golfing and Tennis Facilities

Golfing and Tennis Facilities in the Cayman Islands provide wonderful chances for sports fans to enjoy their favorite hobbies while surrounded by magnificent tropical settings. Here are some highlights and safety precautions for each island:

1. Grand Cayman

Golf: The North Sound Club is a superb 18-hole golf course situated in the northern section of the island. It provides tough courses and spectacular vistas of the Caribbean Sea.

Tennis: The Cayman Islands Tennis Club in South Sound boasts excellent tennis facilities with both clay and hard courts.

Remember to wear suitable footwear and bring your equipment.

2. Cayman Brac

Golf: The Cayman Brac Golf Course is a 9-hole course hidden in the gorgeous surroundings of the island. It provides a laid-back environment and is suited for players of all ability levels.

Tennis: The Brac Reef Beach Resort offers tennis courts accessible to guests. Remember to bring your equipment and follow safety standards.

3. Little Cayman

Golf: Little Cayman does not have a golf course, but tourists may enjoy the peacefulness of the island's natural beauty.

Tennis: Little Cayman does not have specific tennis facilities, however, certain resorts may provide tennis courts for their visitors.

Safety Tips
1. Follow safety rules and recommendations supplied by the facility.
2. Stay hydrated and protect yourself from the sun with sunscreen and suitable gear.
3. Respect the rules of the game and other players' space.
4. Be careful of animals and the environment while playing.

Rock Climbing and Rappelling

Rock climbing and rappelling lovers will find lots of interesting possibilities to face vertical difficulties in the gorgeous surroundings of the Cayman Islands. While the islands may not be renowned for high cliffs, there are still a few sites where first-timers may experience these exhilarating sports.

Grand Cayman: The Mastic Trail features unusual rock formations that enable chances for rock climbing and rappelling. Ensure you have suitable gear and seek help from local adventure businesses for a safe experience.

Cayman Brac: The Bluff in Cayman Brac is a renowned place for rock climbing and rappelling. Its limestone cliffs provide a selection of routes ideal for novices. Always employ correct safety equipment, including helmets and harnesses, and consider hiring a qualified guide.

Little Cayman: Although the alternatives for rock climbing and rappelling are limited in Little Cayman, the island's craggy coastline allows cliffside rappelling. Exercise caution and be attentive to your surroundings.

Safety Tips
1. Always employ adequate safety gear, including helmets, harnesses, and ropes.
2. Ensure you have adequate training and expertise before trying rock climbing and rappelling.
3. Check weather conditions and be mindful of possible risks, such as loose pebbles or slippery surfaces.
4. Respect the environment and observe all local rules and regulations involving rock climbing and rappelling activities.

Beachcombing and Relaxation

When it comes to relaxing and enjoying the tranquility of the beach, the Cayman Islands provide exquisite places throughout its three islands. Let's investigate where you may enjoy beachcombing and leisure while keeping safe and obeying local rules.

Grand Cayman: Seven Mile Beach is a gorgeous length of soft white sand and crystal-clear waters, excellent for strolls and gathering seashells.
Remember to observe any signs respecting protected areas and avoid destroying any natural resources.

Cayman Brac: Head to South Side Public Beach, a peaceful paradise with stunning vistas. Enjoy a relaxing stroll down the coast, soaking in the beauty of the surroundings. Keep in mind that removing living marine creatures or coral is banned.

Little Cayman: Point of Sand Beach is a quiet paradise with clean coastlines and diverse aquatic life. Take a stroll, soak up the sun, and observe the natural beauties surrounding you. Remember to leave everything as you found it to maintain the delicate environment.

Safety Tips
1. Stay hydrated and apply sunscreen to protect yourself from the sun's rays.
2. Respect any signs or cautions about currents or wildlife protection.
3. Dispose of garbage appropriately and keep the beaches clean.
4. It is crucial to remember that removing living marine life, corals, or shells with creatures inside is banned.
5. Be careful of marine conditions and avoid swimming in turbulent seas.
6. Always be alert and attentive to your surroundings.

Bird-watching

Bird-watching in the Cayman Islands is a fascinating experience for nature aficionados.

Here are some suggested sites in each of the islands where first-timers may enjoy this intriguing activity:

Grand Cayman: Queen Elizabeth II Botanic Park: This 65-acre park is a sanctuary for birds, with over 40 species of resident and migratory birds. Explore the wooded paths and wetland areas to view colorful birds like the Caribbean parrot and West Indian whistling duck.

Cayman Brac: Brac Parrot Reserve: Home to the endangered Cayman Brac parrot, this area provides superb birding possibilities. Follow the indicated pathways to witness these lovely birds in their natural environment.

Little Cayman: Booby Pond Nature Reserve: This globally designated Ramsar site is a paradise for birdwatchers. Discover the biggest nesting colony of red-footed boobies in the western hemisphere and discover other bird species including frigatebirds and herons.

Safety Tips
1. Respect animals and their habitats by viewing them from a distance.
2. Stay on approved pathways and avoid harming nests or nesting grounds.
3. Follow local rules and regulations, such as getting licenses for bird photography or handling.
4. Carry binoculars, a field guide, and a camera to maximize your bird viewing experience.

Sunset Cruises

Sunset Cruises in the Cayman Islands provides a spectacular experience, combining stunning views of the setting sun with a relaxing boat cruise. For first-time visitors, here are some wonderful sites to take a sunset sail on each of the islands:

Grand Cayman: Head to Seven Mile Beach or George Town Harbour for a range of sunset boat options. Enjoy the gorgeous coastline and vivid sunsets as you cruise around the western borders of the island.

Cayman Brac: Check out the South Side of Cayman Brac for sunset cruises. The peaceful seas and majestic cliffs create a stunning background as you observe the sun setting beyond the horizon.

Little Cayman: Visit Point of Sand Beach in Little Cayman, recognized for its remote and unspoiled beauty. From here, you may go on a sunset sail, surrounded by unspoiled natural surroundings.

Safety Tips
1. Always use a life jacket and stick to safety rules issued by the cruise operator.
2. Stay hydrated and protect yourself from the sun with sunscreen and suitable gear.
3. Respect the maritime environment and prevent trash.
4. Be careful of local restrictions surrounding alcohol drinking on boats.
5. Listen to the captain's directions and follow any safety precautions.

Stargazing

Stargazing in the Cayman Islands is a beautiful experience that enables you to observe the beauties of the night sky in all its splendor. Whether you're a seasoned stargazer or a first-timer, here are several wonderful sites around the islands where you may enjoy the cosmic beauty:

Grand Cayman: Head to the quiet beaches on the eastern side of the island, such as Rum Point or Starfish Point. These sites have low light pollution and give an unimpeded view of the night sky.

Cayman Brac: Visit the Brac Parrot Reserve or the Bluff regions for an amazing astronomy experience. These lofty sites provide beautiful panoramic vistas and a calm backdrop for studying the stars.

Little Cayman: The virgin beaches of Owen Island or Point of Sand are perfect settings for stargazing. You may discover quiet areas where the lack of city lights allows for good views of the night sky.

Safety Tips
1. Always pack a flashlight with a red filter to maintain your night vision and travel securely.
2. Respect private property and avoid trespassing while seeking stargazing places.
3. Do not trash and leave the environment as you found it to maintain its natural beauty.
4. Be cautious of animals and their habitats when stargazing.

PRACTICAL
INFORMATION

CHAPTER
NINE

Welcome to this chapter of our guidebook, where I provide you with essential practical information for your first-time visit to the Cayman Islands. In this chapter, I'll cover key aspects such as accommodations and transportation, ensuring that you have a smooth and enjoyable experience during your stay.

Finding the right accommodations is crucial for a comfortable and convenient trip. I'll guide you through the various types of accommodations available, including luxury resorts, boutique hotels, vacation rentals, and budget-friendly options, helping you choose the perfect place to suit your preferences and budget.

Transportation is another important consideration, and I'll provide you with insights into the different options available on the islands. Whether you prefer to rent a car and explore at your own pace, rely on taxis for convenience, or utilize public transportation, I'll help you navigate the best transportation methods to get around the islands efficiently.

Transportation in the Cayman Islands

Transportation in the Cayman Islands offers various options to help you explore the islands at your own pace. Here are some key modes of transportation and my insights on each:

1. Rental Cars: Rental car services are available on all three islands. Most rental agencies have convenient opening hours, typically from 8:00 AM to 5:00 PM. Renting a car provides flexibility and allows you to discover the islands independently. The cost varies depending on the type of vehicle and rental duration. The cars are generally well-maintained and comfortable. The drivers are professional and helpful, ensuring a smooth experience. However, be mindful of driving on the left side of the road if you are not accustomed to it.

2. Taxis: Taxis are a popular and readily available option. They operate 24/7, providing convenient transportation at any time. Taxis in the Cayman Islands are known for their safety and reliability. The fare structure is regulated, and rates are fixed per zone or destination. The drivers are professional and knowledgeable about the islands, offering valuable insights and recommendations. Taxis are comfortable and well-maintained. However, the fares can be relatively higher compared to other modes of transportation.

3. Public Transportation: Public buses operate on the larger islands, primarily Grand Cayman. They offer an affordable way to get around, with routes covering major attractions and towns. The buses have fixed schedules and operate from early morning until late evening.
The cost is relatively low, making it a budget-friendly option. However, buses can get crowded during peak hours, affecting comfort. Timeliness may vary, so it's important to plan accordingly.

4. Bike Rentals: Bike rentals are available on the islands, offering a unique way to explore at a leisurely pace. The opening hours vary depending on the rental shop. Biking allows you to enjoy the scenic beauty of the islands and offers a great sense of freedom. However, be cautious of traffic and ensure road safety while cycling.

5. Rental Cars: Renting a car gives you the freedom to explore the islands at your own pace. Rental agencies have a wide range of vehicles to choose from, and they usually offer flexible opening hours. Driving in the Cayman Islands is on the left side of the road, similar to the UK and other British territories. It's important to note that rush hour traffic can be congested in urban areas. Make sure to go along with a valid driver's license and ID.

6. Water Taxis: Water taxis are a convenient and enjoyable mode of transportation in the Cayman Islands, particularly for island hopping or coastal exploration. These boats provide a unique way to travel between islands or along the picturesque coastline, offering stunning views of crystal-clear waters.

Water taxis are typically privately owned and operated, and you can find them at designated docks or marinas. They offer flexible schedules and can often be chartered for private tours or customized trips.
The captains of water taxis are experienced and knowledgeable about the surrounding waters, ensuring a safe and smooth journey.

One of the advantages of using water taxis is the ability to avoid traffic and enjoy a more relaxed and scenic ride. You can sit back, relax, and take in the breathtaking sights as you cruise along the coast or between the islands.

While water taxis can be more expensive compared to other forms of transportation, the unique experience and convenience they offer make them worth considering, especially for special occasions or when you want to make the most of your time exploring the islands.

It's important to note that water taxi availability and operating hours may vary, so it's advisable to check in advance or make reservations if necessary. Additionally, be mindful of any safety instructions provided by the water taxi operators and follow their guidelines for a pleasant and secure journey.

7. Scooter Rentals: Scooter rentals are a popular and convenient transportation option for exploring the Cayman Islands at your own pace. Renting a scooter gives you the freedom to navigate the islands easily and discover hidden gems that may be off the beaten path.

Scooter rental shops can be found in various locations across the islands, and they typically offer a range of scooter models to suit different preferences and riding abilities. You can choose from manual or automatic scooters, depending on your comfort and experience level.

Renting a scooter allows you to maneuver through traffic and find parking more easily compared to larger vehicles. It also provides a thrilling and immersive way to experience the stunning landscapes and coastal roads of the Cayman Islands.

Before renting a scooter, it's important to ensure you have a valid driver's license that permits you to operate a scooter. Some rental companies may also require you to provide a deposit or proof of insurance.

While scooter rentals offer flexibility and convenience, it's crucial to prioritize safety. Always wear a helmet, follow traffic rules and regulations, and familiarize yourself with the local driving conditions. Be cautious of road conditions, especially during rainy weather, and maintain a defensive riding approach.

The cost of scooter rentals may vary depending on the duration of the rental and the type of scooter chosen. It's recommended to compare prices from different rental shops and read reviews to ensure a reputable and reliable rental experience.

In terms of safety, the Cayman Islands have well-maintained roads and generally adhere to traffic regulations. However, it's essential to practice caution and follow local driving rules. Taxis and rental cars are generally considered safe and reliable.

In my opinion, I find taxis to be a convenient and comfortable option for shorter trips, especially when I want to sit back and relax while enjoying the scenic views.

Rental cars offer flexibility and independence, allowing me to explore hidden gems at my own pace. Public transportation can be an economical choice, but it requires careful planning and patience.

To access transportation services, you can easily find taxi stands at popular tourist spots and near major hotels. Rental car agencies are located at airports and in urban areas. Public bus stops are marked, and schedules are available online or at designated stops.

Accommodation Options

From luxury resorts to cozy guesthouses, the Cayman Islands offer a wide range of accommodation options to suit every traveler's needs.

Luxury Resorts and Hotels

The Ritz-Carlton, Grand Cayman: A world-class resort offering elegant accommodations, stunning ocean views, and impeccable service. It is close to Camana Bay and Cayman Turtle Center.

Location: Seven Mile Beach, Grand Cayman

Opening and Closing Hours: 24 hours

View: Breathtaking views of the Caribbean Sea

Services: Spa, fitness center, multiple dining options, concierge services

Room Types and Costs: Deluxe Room starting at $500 per night, Oceanfront Suite starting at $1,000 per night

Staff Attitude: Friendly and attentive

Rating: 5 out of 5 stars

Positive: Luxurious amenities, beautiful beachfront location

Negative: Higher price range

Dressing Requirements: Resort casual

Kids and Pets: Family-friendly, pets not allowed

Visitors Rules and Etiquettes: Respectful behavior towards other guests and staff

Payment Options: Credit cards accepted

Amenities: Outdoor pool, tennis courts, water sports, kids' club

Transportation: Shuttle service available

Reservation: Reservations can be made online on their official

website:
www.ritzcarlton.com/grandcayman

2. Le Soleil d'Or, Cayman Brac
An exclusive boutique hotel nestled in a tropical paradise with lush gardens and private beach access. It is close to Cayman Brac Museum and the Bluff.

Location: South Side Road, Cayman Brac

Opening and Closing Hours: 24 hours

View: Beautiful views of the Caribbean Sea and gardens

Services: Spa, farm-to-table dining, concierge services

Room Types and Costs: Garden Cottage starting at $400 per night, Beachfront Villa starting at $800 per night

Staff Attitude: Warm and attentive

Rating: 4.5 out of 5 stars

Positive: Tranquil setting, farm-fresh cuisine

Negative: Limited dining options nearby

Dressing Requirements: Resort casual

Kids and Pets: Family-friendly, pets not allowed

Visitors Rules and Etiquettes: Respectful behavior towards other guests and staff

Payment Options: Credit cards accepted

Amenities: Private beach, swimming pool, fitness center, yoga classes

Transportation: Car rental recommended

Reservation: Reservations can be made online on their official

website:
www.lesoleildor.com

3. The Club at Little Cayman
A secluded paradise offering upscale accommodations and a serene atmosphere. Close to Bloody Bay Marine Park and Point of Sand Beach.

Location: Blossom Village, Little Cayman

Opening and Closing Hours: 24 hours

View: Spectacular views of the Caribbean Sea

Services: Dive center, restaurant, bar, concierge services

Room Types and Costs: Ocean View Suite starting at $600 per night, Beachfront Bungalow starting at $900 per night

Staff Attitude: Friendly and helpful

Rating: 4 out of 5 stars

Positive: Pristine beachfront location, excellent diving opportunities

Negative: Limited dining options on-site

Dressing Requirements: Resort casual

Kids and Pets: Adults-only resort, no pets allowed

Visitors Rules and Etiquettes: Respectful behavior towards other guests and staff

Payment Options: Credit cards accepted

Amenities: Outdoor pool, private beach cabanas, yoga studio

Transportation: Bicycle rentals are available

Reservation: Reservations can be made online on their official

website:
www.clubatlittlecayman.com

Boutique & Eco-Friendly Lodgings

1. Grand Cayman: Serenity Eco-Lodge

Serenity Eco-Lodge provides a tranquil and eco-conscious getaway, surrounded by beautiful tropical gardens. The resort prides itself on sustainability, embracing solar electricity and eco-friendly techniques.

Location: Situated on the calm sands of Seven Mile Beach, Grand Cayman.

Close by landmarks: Close to Camana Bay and the Cayman Turtle Centre.

Opening and closing hours: Open 24/7.

View: Enjoy magnificent views of the Caribbean Sea from your accommodation or the lodge's beach.

Services: Personalized concierge service, eco-tours, yoga lessons, and spa treatments.

Room types and costs: Choose from eco-friendly cottages or luxurious suites, beginning at $200 per night.

Staff attitude: Friendly and attentive, offering a warm and welcoming atmosphere.

Rating: Highly praised for its devotion to sustainability and tranquility.

Positive aspects: Stunning beachside setting, eco-conscious facilities, and customized service.

Negative aspects: Limited on-site eating alternatives.

Dressing requirements: Casual attire.

Kids and dogs permitted: Family-friendly and pets may be allowed with prior agreement.

Visitors' norms and etiquettes: Respect the natural environment and stick to eco-friendly principles.

Payment options: Credit cards accepted; online booking available.

Amenities: Beach access, on-site restaurant, spa, eco-friendly amenities.

Reservation: Reservations may be made online via their official

website:
www.serenityecolodge.com

2. Cayman Brac: Harmony Retreat
Harmony Retreat provides a tranquil and private location, surrounded by tropical vegetation and animals. The resort incorporates sustainable techniques and gives a tranquil getaway from the hectic world.

Location: Nestled among the rugged beauty of Cayman Brac.

Close by landmarks: Near the Bluff and the Brac Parrot Reserve.

Opening and closing hours: Open from 8 AM to 10 PM.

View: Enjoy stunning views of the Caribbean Sea and the island's natural scenery.

Services: Relaxing spa treatments, yoga classes, guided nature walks, and individualized wellness programs.

Room types and costs: Choose from modest eco-cottages or luxurious treehouses, beginning at $150 per night.

Staff attitude: Warm and attentive, delivering customized service and a cheerful environment.

Rating: Highly praised for its natural surroundings, tranquility, and wellness options.

Positive aspects: Serene environment, eco-friendly accommodation, and relaxing wellness activities.

Negative aspects: Limited food alternatives within walking distance.

Dressing requirements: Casual attire.

Kids and dogs permitted: Family-friendly and pets may be allowed with prior agreement.

Visitors' regulations & etiquette: Respect the natural surroundings and preserve a tranquil environment.

Payment options: Credit cards accepted; online booking available.

Amenities: Spa, yoga deck, wildlife paths.

Reservation: Reservations may be made via their official

website:
www.harmonyretreat.com

3. Little Cayman: Paradise Cove Resort

Paradise Cove Resort provides a serene and eco-friendly vacation, surrounded by stunning white sand beaches and crystal-clear seas. The resort is devoted to sustainability and conserving the natural beauty of the island.

Location: Nestled on the peaceful coastline of Little Cayman.

Close by landmarks: Near the Booby Pond Nature Reserve and Point of Sand Beach.

Opening and closing hours: Open 24/7.

View: Enjoy magnificent views of the Caribbean Sea and the resort's beach.

Services: Dive trips, snorkeling tours, bike rentals, and beachside massages.

Room types and costs: Choose from beachfront cottages or ocean-view suites, beginning at $250 per night.

Staff attitude: Friendly and helpful, creating a wonderful stay for customers.

Rating: Highly praised for its magnificent setting, eco-friendly efforts, and attentive personnel.

Positive aspects: Idyllic beachside environment, superb diving and snorkeling chances, and eco-conscious methods.

Negative aspects: Limited food alternatives on-site.

Dressing requirements: Casual attire.

Kids and dogs permitted: Family-friendly and pets may be allowed with prior agreement.

Visitors' norms and etiquettes: Respect the natural environment and stick to eco-friendly principles.

Payment options: Credit cards accepted; online booking available.

Amenities: Beach access, on-site restaurant, diving center, spa services.

Reservation: Reservations may be made via their official

website:
www.paradisecoveresort.com

Budget-Friendly Accommodations

1. Grand Cayman: Coral Sands Resort
Coral Sands Resort provides comfortable and reasonable lodgings only steps away from the magnificent beach. The resort offers a relaxing environment and quick access to neighboring attractions.

Location: Located in the center of Seven Mile Beach, Grand Cayman.

Close by landmarks: Close to Camana Bay and the Cayman Turtle Centre.

Opening and closing hours: Open 24/7.

View: Enjoy partial views of the Caribbean Sea or the resort's tropical gardens.

Services: Daily cleaning, front desk help, and tour booking.

Types of rooms and costs: Choose from regular rooms or suites, beginning at $100 per night.

Staff attitude: Friendly and helpful, offering a welcoming atmosphere for visitors.

Rating: Rated as a budget-friendly alternative with decent facilities and services.

Positive aspects: Affordable pricing, accessibility to the beach, and pleasant personnel.

Negative aspects: Limited on-site facilities.

Dressing requirements: Casual attire.

Kids and dogs permitted: Family-friendly and pets may be allowed with prior agreement.

Visitors' norms and etiquette: Respect fellow guests and adhere to the resort's standards.

Payment options: Credit cards accepted; online booking available.

Amenities: Beach access, free Wi-Fi, on-site restaurant.

Reservation: Reservations may be made online via their official

website:
www.coralsands.com

2. Cayman Brac: Brac Caribbean Beach Village

Brac Caribbean Beach Village provides cheap beachfront villas surrounded by natural beauty. The community offers a tranquil and laid-back environment for tourists to enjoy their stay.

Location: Situated on the gorgeous coastline of Cayman Brac.

Close by landmarks: Near the Bluff and the Brac Parrot Reserve.

Opening and closing hours: Open 24/7.

View: Enjoy amazing views of the Caribbean Sea from your cottage.

Services: Daily cleaning, front desk help, and bicycle rentals.

Types of rooms and costs: Choose from beachfront cottages or garden-view rooms, beginning at $80 per night.

Staff attitude: Friendly and helpful, offering a great stay for customers.

Rating: Rated as a budget-friendly alternative with a relaxing ambiance.

Positive aspects: Affordable prices, beachside location, and nice personnel.

Negative aspects: Limited food alternatives within walking distance.

Dressing requirements: Casual attire.

Kids and dogs permitted: Family-friendly and pets may be allowed with prior agreement.

Visitors' regulations & etiquette: Respect the natural surroundings and preserve a tranquil environment.

Payment options: Credit cards accepted; online booking available.

Amenities: Beach access, free Wi-Fi, outdoor lounging spaces.

Reservation: Reservations may be made online using their

website:
www.bracbeachvillage.com

3. Little Cayman: Paradise Palms Bed and Breakfast

Paradise Palms Bed & Breakfast provides inexpensive and comfortable rooms in a gorgeous tropical location. The B&B offers a comfortable setting and individual treatment for visitors.

Location: Located in a calm part of Little Cayman.

Close by landmarks: Near the Booby Pond Nature Reserve and Point of Sand Beach.

Opening and closing hours: Open 24/7.

View: Enjoy views of the magnificent gardens and adjacent natural settings.

Services: Daily breakfast, trip information, and help with activity arrangements.

Types of rooms and costs: Choose from guest rooms with shared amenities, beginning at $60 per night.

Staff attitude: Friendly and attentive, guaranteeing a nice stay for visitors.

Rating: Rated as a budget-friendly alternative with a comfortable environment.

Positive aspects: Affordable pricing, calm atmosphere, and individual service.

Negative aspects: Limited on-site facilities.

Dressing requirements: Casual attire.

Kids and dogs permitted: Family-friendly and pets may be allowed with prior agreement.

Visitors' norms and etiquettes: Respect other visitors' privacy and promote a pleasant atmosphere.

Payment options: Cash or credit cards are accepted.

Amenities: Complimentary breakfast, community kitchen, outdoor lounging spaces.

Reservation: Reservations may be made by contacting the resort directly via
website:
www.paradisepalms.com.

Vacation Rentals and Villas

1. Grand Cayman: Sunset Paradise Villas
Sunset Paradise Villas provides magnificent beachfront villas with amazing sunset views. The villas are attractively built and furnished with contemporary conveniences for a pleasant stay.

Location: Seven Mile Beach, Grand Cayman.

Close by landmarks: Close to Camana Bay and Cayman Turtle Centre.

Opening and closing hours: Open 24/7.

View: Enjoy amazing views of the Caribbean Sea and immediate access to Seven Mile Beach.

Services: Housekeeping, concierge service, and on-site maintenance.

Types of rooms and costs: Choose from large one to four-bedroom villas, beginning at $400 per night.

Staff attitude: Professional and attentive, offering a smooth stay for visitors.

Rating: Highly regarded for its seaside setting, lavish facilities, and responsive personnel.

Positive aspects: Stunning beachside location, well-appointed homes, and outstanding customer service.

Negative aspects: Limited food alternatives within walking distance.

Dressing requirements: Casual attire.

Kids and dogs permitted: Family-friendly and pets may be allowed with prior agreement.

Visitors' norms and etiquettes: Respect the property and create a pleasant environment.

Payment options: Credit cards accepted; online booking available.

Amenities: Beach access, private pool, fully supplied kitchen, Wi-Fi, parking.

Reservation: Reservations may be made online using their

website:
www.sunsetparadisevillas.com
phone:
+1 345-555-1234.

2. Cayman Brac: Brac Caribbean Beach Village
Brac Caribbean Beach Village provides lovely beachfront bungalows with a relaxing island ambiance. The cottages are surrounded by beautiful gardens and offer a calm hideaway on Cayman Brac.

Location: South Side, Cayman Brac.

Close by landmarks: Near the Bluff and Brac Parrot Reserve.

Reservation: Reservations may be made via their official

website:
www.bracbeachvillage.com.
phone :
+1 345-555-5678.

3. Little Cayman: Tranquility Bay Beach House

Tranquility Bay Beach House is a lovely beachfront vacation property giving a calm and private respite. The beach house offers a peaceful and pleasant refuge in Little Cayman.

Location: Blossom Village, Little Cayman.

Close by landmarks: Near the Booby Pond Nature Reserve and Point of Sand Beach.

Opening and closing hours: Open 24/7.

View: Enjoy spectacular views of the Caribbean Sea and immediate beach access.

Services: Housekeeping, property management, and help with island activities.

Types of rooms and costs: A big three-bedroom beach home, beginning at $350 per night.

Staff attitude: Friendly and responsive, offering a nice stay for customers.

Rating: Highly regarded for its tranquil location, coastal setting, and attentive service.

Positive aspects: Secluded seaside location, roomy accommodation, and courteous personnel.

Negative aspects: Limited food alternatives within walking distance.

Dressing requirements: Casual attire.

Kids and dogs permitted: Family-friendly and pets may be allowed with prior agreement.

Visitors' regulations and etiquette: Respect the property and create a pleasant environment.

Payment options: Credit cards accepted; online booking available.

Amenities: Beach access, fully equipped kitchen, outdoor sitting, Wi-Fi, parking.

Reservation: Reservations may be made via their official

website:
www.tranquilitybaybeachhouse.com
phone:
+1 345-555-9012.

Camping and Outdoor Accommodations

1. Grand Cayman: Sunset Bay Camping

Sunset Bay Camping gives a picturesque camping experience with spectacular sunset views over the Caribbean Sea. Set up your tent or bring your RV and enjoy the natural beauty of the island.

Location: Situated on the gorgeous coastline of Grand Cayman.

Close by landmarks: Close to Seven Mile Beach and the Cayman Turtle Centre.

Opening and closing hours: Open 24/7.

View: Enjoy spectacular views of the sunset and the glittering ocean.

Services: Basic camping amenities include restrooms, showers, and picnic sites.

Types of lodgings and costs: Bring your tent or RV. Tent sites start at $20 per night.

Staff attitude: Friendly and helpful, offering a great camping experience.

Rating: Rated as a budget-friendly camping choice with wonderful views.

Positive aspects: Scenic setting, inexpensive prices, and near access to famous attractions.

Negative aspects: Limited amenities and facilities.

Dressing requirements: Casual clothes suited for camping.

Kids and dogs permitted: Family-friendly and pets may be allowed with prior agreement.

Visitors' norms and etiquettes: Respect quiet hours, maintain the camping area clean, and respect campsite laws.

Payment options: Cash or credit cards may be accepted on-site.

Amenities: Restrooms, showers, picnic sites.

Reservation: Reservations may not be necessary, since spots are available on a first-come, first-served basis.

2. Cayman Brac: Brac Reef Camping

Brac Reef Camping provides a calm camping experience within the natural beauty of the island. Set your tent and enjoy the gorgeous sceneries, including cliffs and pristine beaches.

Location: Located on the picturesque Cayman Brac.

Close by landmarks: Near the Bluff and the Brac Parrot Reserve.

Opening and closing hours: Open 24/7.

View: Enjoy magnificent views of the Caribbean Sea and the island's natural environs.

Services: Basic camping amenities include bathrooms, outdoor grills, and picnic spots.

Types of lodgings and costs: Bring your tent. Tent sites start at $25 per night.

Staff attitude: Welcoming and helpful, giving aid as required.

Rating: Rated as a calm camping location with excellent views of the ocean.

Positive aspects: Serene environment, natural surroundings, and inexpensive pricing.

Negative aspects: Limited facilities and services.

Dressing requirements: Casual clothes suited for camping.

Kids and dogs permitted: Family-friendly and pets may be allowed with prior agreement.

Visitors' norms and etiquette: Respect the environment, keep the camping area clean, and obey campground rules.

Payment options: Cash or credit cards may be accepted on-site.

Amenities: Restrooms, outdoor grills, picnic sites.

Reservation: Reservations may not be necessary, since spots are available on a first-come, first-served basis.

3. Little Cayman: Paradise Cove Camping
Paradise Cove Camping provides a private and gorgeous camping experience on the lovely island of Little Cayman. Immerse yourself in the natural beauty and calm of the surroundings.

Location: Nestled on the gorgeous coastline of Little Cayman.

Close by landmarks: Near the Booby Pond Nature Reserve and Point of Sand Beach.

Opening and closing hours: Open 24/7.

View: Enjoy amazing views of the Caribbean Sea and the beautiful sandy beach.

Services: Basic camping amenities include restrooms, outdoor showers, and shared fire pits.

Types of lodgings and costs: Bring your tent. Tent sites start at $30 per night.

Staff attitude: Friendly and helpful, offering a great camping experience.

Rating: Rated as a tranquil and lovely camping location with wonderful ocean views.

Positive aspects: Pristine beachside setting, serene ambiance, and natural surroundings.

Negative aspects: Limited facilities and services.

Dressing requirements: Casual clothes suited for camping.

Kids and dogs permitted: Family-friendly and pets may be allowed with prior agreement.

Visitors' norms and etiquette: Respect the environment, keep the camping area clean, and obey campground rules.

Payment options: Cash or credit cards may be accepted on-site.

Amenities: Restrooms, outdoor showers, community fire pits.

Reservation: Reservations may not be necessary, since spots are available on a first-come, first-served basis.

INSIDER TIPS
&
RECOMMENDATIONS

CHAPTER 10

As a seasoned tourist to the Cayman Islands, I'm glad to provide insider ideas and suggestions for you. In this chapter, I'll take you beyond the well-trodden routes and find the hidden jewels that make the Cayman Islands so remarkable.

To thoroughly immerse oneself in the local culture, I'll share vital insights into Caymanian traditions and etiquette. Learn about the island's warm hospitality, traditional greetings, and dining etiquette to guarantee a polite and delightful experience throughout your visit.

Safety is crucial, so I'll give critical suggestions and safeguards to keep you well-informed and prepared. From water safety rules to tips on coping with tropical weather conditions, you'll have the expertise to handle your experiences with confidence.

Get ready to learn the mysteries of the Cayman Islands and make amazing experiences as you embrace the hidden treasures and immerse yourself in the native way of life. Let's go on this voyage of discovery together!

Local Customs and Etiquette

When visiting the Cayman Islands, it's crucial to educate oneself about the local traditions and etiquette to guarantee a courteous and pleasurable stay. Here are some crucial traditions and manners to bear in mind:

1. Greetings: Caymanians are recognized for their warm and welcoming disposition. When greeting someone, a handshake, and a polite grin are acceptable. It is usual to greet someone with a warm "hello" or "good day."

2. Dress Code: The Cayman Islands offer a relaxed and informal environment, yet it is vital to dress correctly in particular circumstances.

When visiting religious locations or luxury restaurants, it's wise to dress modestly. Beachwear is permissible on the beaches but should be covered while visiting other facilities.

3. Tipping: Tipping is traditional in the Cayman Islands. In restaurants, a 15-20% tip is usual if a service fee is not already included. For other services, such as cabs or tour guides, a 10-15% tip is recommended.

4. Civility and Respect: Caymanians cherish civility and respect. It is necessary to use "please" and "thank you" while speaking with natives. Be cognizant of cultural differences and avoid sensitive issues in discussion.

5. Punctuality: Being punctual is highly prized in Caymanian society. It is considered respectable to come on time for planned appointments, meetings, or social functions.

6. Beach Etiquette: When visiting the wonderful beaches of the Cayman Islands, remember to respect the environment and other beachgoers. Dispose of your garbage appropriately, prevent excessive noise, and respect any stated laws or restrictions.

7. Conservation and Wildlife: The Cayman Islands are noted for their pristine natural environment. It is crucial to conserve sensitive ecosystems and appreciate the local fauna. Avoid touching or disturbing marine animals, and do not trash or destroy coral reefs.

8. Driving: If you want to drive in the Cayman Islands, be advised that traffic drives on the left-hand side of the road. Observe speed restrictions and be respectful to other cars on the road.

Safety Tips and Precautions

When coming to the Cayman Islands as a first-time tourist, it's crucial to emphasize your safety and well-being. Here are some crucial safety recommendations and measures to keep in mind:

1. Water Safety: The seas around the Cayman Islands are famous for their beauty and recreational options. However, always take care while swimming, snorkeling, or indulging in aquatic activities. Pay heed to any caution flags or signs on the beach, and be aware of strong currents or rough waves. It's advised to swim in authorized areas and follow the directions of lifeguards if available.

2. Sun Protection: The Cayman Islands have a tropical environment with plentiful sunlight. Protect yourself from the sun's rays by wearing sunscreen with a high SPF, a wide-brimmed hat, sunglasses, and lightweight, breathable clothes. Stay hydrated by drinking lots of water throughout the day.

3. Mosquito Protection: Like many tropical places, mosquitoes are found in the Cayman Islands.
To protect yourself against mosquito-borne diseases, such as dengue or Zika, apply insect repellent containing DEET, wear long sleeves and trousers between dawn and twilight, and consider staying in lodgings with screened windows or utilizing mosquito nets.

4. Personal things: Keep a watchful check on your things at all times, particularly in busy locations or tourist sites. Avoid exhibiting precious goods publicly and use a lockable bag or wallet to keep your valuables. It's also advisable to create copies of crucial travel papers and store them separately from the originals.

5. Do not drink the tap water: The tap water in the Cayman Islands is not safe to drink.

Bottled water is accessible everywhere, so make sure to drink bottled water instead of tap water.

6. Be careful of the dress code: The Cayman Islands is a casual location, however, there are certain areas where a more formal dress code is necessary. Be cautious to verify the dress code before attending any restaurants or clubs.

7. Road Safety: If you intend to hire a car or utilize local transit, educate yourself about local traffic laws and regulations. Be careful while crossing roads and always use approved pedestrian crossings. Keep your car secured and windows closed while parked, and avoid leaving valuables unattended.

8. Emergency agencies: Save emergency contact numbers, including the local police and medical agencies, on your phone or write them down for easy access. In case of an emergency, don't hesitate to seek aid or call the proper authorities.

9. Pack for all sorts of weather: The Cayman Islands has a tropical environment, but it may also experience hurricanes and other tropical storms. Be careful to prepare for all sorts of weather, including rain, sun, and wind.

10. Natural Hazards: The Cayman Islands are typically safe from natural catastrophes, but it's crucial to be updated about weather conditions and heed any guidelines or warnings provided by local authorities. In the case of extreme weather, such as hurricanes, follow the directions given by your lodgings or local emergency services.

By being alert, prepared, and observant of these safety guidelines and measures, you may assure a secure and worry-free experience while touring the beautiful Cayman Islands.

APPENDIX

7 Days Suggested Itinerary

DAY 1

MORNING
Start your day with a visit to Stingray City, a sandbar where you may swim with friendly stingrays in their native environment. Afterward, travel to Starfish Point, a remote beach that is home to a variety of starfish.

AFTERNOON
Relax at Rum Point, a gorgeous beach that offers a range of water activities, including snorkeling and kayaking. Grab a bite to eat at the Rum Point Club Restaurant, which provides both vegetarian and seafood choices with spectacular views of the Caribbean Sea.

EVENING
Explore the capital city of Georgetown, which provides a variety of stores, restaurants, and cultural activities. Stop at Hell, a spectacular geological structure that exhibits black limestone formations, before traveling back to your hotel.

DAY 2

MORNING
Visit Seven Mile Beach, one of the most renowned beaches in the world, and soak in the sun on beautiful white sand beaches. Afterward, proceed to Pedro St. James Castle, a restored 18th-century plantation mansion that looks into the island's past.

AFTERNOON
Explore the Queen Elizabeth II Botanic Park, which offers a range of native and exotic flora, as well as an orchid garden and a blue iguana habitat. Stop by Cayman Spirits Co., a local distillery that makes premium rum, for a tour and sampling.

EVENING

Spend the evening in Barker s National Park, a protected area that is home to a variety of animals, including birds and sea turtles. Grab a vegetarian meal at The Brasserie, which provides farm-to-table food in a pleasant ambiance.

DAY 3

MORNING

Visit the Cayman Islands National Museum, which displays the history and culture of the Cayman Islands. Afterward, take a journey to the Underground Pirates Tunnels Bodden Town, a network of tunnels that were formerly utilized by pirates to store their wealth.

AFTERNOON

Relax at Royal Palms Beach Club, a beachside bar and restaurant that provides a choice of food and drink options, as well as spectacular views of the Caribbean Sea. Afterward, travel to Over the Edge Cafe, a local favorite that provides both vegetarian and seafood choices, for supper.

EVENING

Take a journey to West Bay, a calm and lovely community that is home to a variety of stores and eateries. End your night with a visit to the Grand Cayman Seaworld Observatory, a unique underwater observatory that gives a close-up look at the island's aquatic life.

DAY 4

MORNING

Take a day excursion to Cayman Brac Island, a smaller and more isolated island that is recognized for its natural beauty and outdoor activities.

Take a tour of the island and explore its various attractions, including the Atlantis Submarine Center and the Kittiwake Shipwreck & Artificial Reef.

AFTERNOON
Visit the Tortuga Rum Cakes Bakery, where you may try and buy a variety of rum cakes and other local goodies. Afterward, drive back to Grand Cayman and visit the George Town Cruise Port, which offers a variety of stores and eateries.

EVENING
Spend your evening in Camana Bay, a busy beachfront village that has a variety of shops, restaurants, and entertainment opportunities. Grab a seafood meal at Blue by Eric Ripert, which provides fresh seafood and magnificent views of the harbor.

DAY 5

MORNING
Visit the Mastic Reserve & Trail, an 834-acre natural reserve that provides hiking paths, birding, and breathtaking views of the island's flora and animals. Afterward, proceed to the Cayman Turtle Centre, which is home to a variety of sea turtles, as well as other marine animals.

AFTERNOON
Relax on the beach at Smith Cove, a private cove that has crystal-clear water and breathtaking vistas. Grab a vegetarian lunch at Bread and Chocolate, a quaint bistro that provides a range of veggie-friendly alternatives.

EVENING
Spend your evening at Kaibo Beach Bar and Grill, a beachside restaurant that provides a choice of seafood and vegetarian options, as well as live music and entertainment.

DAY 6

MORNING
Explore the Crystal Tunnels, a network of subterranean tunnels that are home to crystal-clear water and magnificent structures. Afterward, travel to the Cayman Islands Yacht Club, where you may hire a boat or take a sailing lesson.

AFTERNOON
Visit the Cayman Islands Brewery (Caybrew), which provides a range of locally made beers, for a tour and tasting. Afterward, walk to the Lobster Pot Restaurant and Wine Bar, a local favorite that provides fresh seafood and a wide wine selection.

EVENING
Spend your final night in the Cayman Islands resting at your hotel or enjoying a leisurely walk along the beach.

DAY 7

Departure: Reflect on your journey and the experiences you've created before leaving back home.

Extra Health and Safety Information

The Cayman Islands is a generally secure destination to visit, but there are a few health and safety issues that you should be aware of.

Crime
Crime rates are low in the Cayman Islands, however, minor theft and break-ins do occur. You should take the normal steps to safeguard your things, such as:
1. Do not leave valuables unattended.
2. Lock your hotel room door as you leave.
3. Be alert of your surroundings while you are out and about.

Scuba Diving and Snorkeling

The Cayman Islands are a popular location for scuba diving and snorkeling. However, there are a few hazards linked with these activities that you should be aware of:

1. Decompression sickness (the bends): This is a dangerous ailment that may develop if you rise too soon after diving.

2. Aquatic life: There are a variety of aquatic species in the Cayman Islands that may be destructive, such as sharks, stingrays, and jellyfish.

3. Currents: The currents in the Cayman Islands may be powerful, therefore it is vital to be aware of them and to swim in regions that are shielded from the currents.

Drowning

Drowning is a significant cause of death in the Cayman Islands. It is crucial to be informed of the hazards of drowning and to take efforts to avoid it, such as:

1. Always swim with a partner.
2. Do not swim in regions that are known to be harmful, such as locations with strong currents or rip tides.
3. Do not swim if you are inebriated.

Heat Stroke

The Cayman Islands are a tropical vacation, thus it is vital to be mindful of the hazards of heat stroke. Heat stroke is a dangerous ailment that may develop if you are not well-hydrated. To avoid heat stroke, you should:

1. Drink lots of fluids.
2. Avoid vigorous activities during the warmest portion of the day.
3. Wear loose-fitting, light-colored apparel.

4. Apply sunscreen to exposed skin.

Sunburn
The Cayman Islands are a sunny location, thus it is necessary to be aware of the hazards of sunburn. Sunburn may cause discomfort, redness, and burning. To avoid sunburn, you should:

1. Wear sunscreen with an SPF of 30 or higher.
2. Reapply sunscreen every two hours, or more frequently if you are exercising or swimming.
3. Wear a hat and sunglasses.
4. Avoid being in the sun during the warmest portion of the day.

Basic Phrases in Cayman Creole

Here are some basic phrases in Cayman Creole:
Hello: Howdy or Wah gwaan (pronounced "wah gwon")
Goodbye: See ye
Good afternoon: Gud aftanoon
Good evening: Gud evenin
Yes: Ya
No: Nah
Please: Please
Thank you: Tanks
You're welcome: No problem
Excuse me: Scuse me
How are you?: How yuh deh? (pronounced "how yuh deh")
I'm fine: Mi fine.
Do you speak English?: Yu spik English?
I don't speak Cayman Creole: Mi no spik Cayman Creole.
I don't understand: Mi noh undastan
Can you help me?: Can yu help me?
I'm lost: Mi lost.
Can you tell me where the nearest bathroom is?: Can yu tell me where da nex' bahroom deh?

Can you recommend a good restaurant?: Can yu recommend a good res'ren'?
How much does this cost?: How much da dis cost?
I'd like to buy this: Mi want to buy dis.
That's all: Dat's all.
Do you have any discounts?: Yu got any discounts?
Can I get a receipt?: Can mi get a receipt?
What is your name?: Waa yuh nyam?
My name is…: Mi nyam...
Where is...?: Wey...deh?
Remember, Cayman Creole is a unique dialect spoken in the Cayman Islands. These phrases will help you engage with locals and show your interest in their culture.

Emergency Contacts

Here are some of the most important emergency contacts in the Cayman Islands:
Police: 911
Fire: 911
Ambulance: 911
Coast Guard: 911
Poison Control: 949-7774
Mental Health Crisis Line: 949-8395
Domestic Violence Hotline: 949-7779
Sexual Assault Hotline: 949-7779
Child Abuse Hotline: 949-7779
Tourist Information: 949-7777

It is crucial to keep a list of these contacts with you at all times when in the Cayman Islands. This will assist you to acquire the support that you need in an emergency.

Downloadable & Printable Cayman Islands Maps

To download and print maps of the Cayman Islands, you may follow these procedures using several map services:

Google Maps

a. Open Google Maps on your PC or mobile device.

b. Search for "Cayman Islands" or the precise place you wish to download.

c. Once the map is shown, click on the menu button (three horizontal lines) in the upper left corner.

d. Select "Offline maps" from the menu.

e. Tap on "Custom map" and adjust the region you wish to download by zooming in or out.

f. Tap on "Download" to store the map for offline usage.

g. Connect your device to a printer and print the downloaded map.

OpenStreetMap

a. Visit the OpenStreetMap website (www.openstreetmap.org) on your PC.

b. Search for "Cayman Islands" or the precise place you wish to download.

c. Zoom in or out to alter the map view.

d. Click on the "Export" icon in the upper left corner.

e. Choose the format you choose (e.g., PDF) and pick the required resolution.

f. Click on "Export" to get the map file.

g. Open the downloaded file and print it using a printer.

Maps.me

a. Install the Maps.me app on your mobile device from the App Store or Google Play Store.

b. Open the app and search for "Cayman Islands" or the precise location you wish to download.

c. Once the map is shown, tap on the menu button (three horizontal lines) in the upper left corner.

d. Select "Download maps" from the menu.

e. Adjust the region you wish to download by zooming in or out.

f. Tap on "Download" to store the map for offline usage.

g. Connect your mobile device to a printer and print the downloaded map.

Paper Maps
1. Purchase a paper map of the Cayman Islands from a bookshop, travel agency, or internet vendor.
2. Open the map and locate the required place.
3. Use a pen or pencil to note the place.
4. Fold the map and carry it with you on your vacation.

Once you have downloaded or bought a map of the Cayman Islands, you can print it off using a regular printer.

Here are some suggestions for printing maps:
1. Use a high-quality printer: A high-quality printer will create a better-quality map.
2. Use high-quality paper: High-quality paper will assist to keep the map from curling or wrinkling.
3. Set the printer to print at its maximum resolution: This will generate a crisper picture.
4. Print the map on a big sheet of paper: This will help you to see more information on the map.

By following these instructions, you may download and print maps of the Cayman Islands using popular map sites like Google Maps, OpenStreetMap, and Maps.me. This will enable you to have a tangible copy of the map for convenient reference throughout your stay.

Packing List and Essentials

Here's a packing list for a trip to the Cayman Islands:
1. Clothing:
- Lightweight and breathable clothing for warm weather.
- Swimwear and beach cover-ups.
- Hats, sunglasses, and sunscreen for sun protection.
- Comfortable walking shoes and sandals.
- Light jackets and cardigans for cooler evenings.

2. Travel Documents:
- Valid passport
- Printed or digital copies of flight tickets, hotel reservations, and travel insurance.
- Important visas, driving license, IDs and permits.

3. Electronics and gadgets:
- Camera or smart phone with good quality for nice photos.
- Portable charger.
- Travel adapter to charge your electronics.

4. Beach Essentials:
- Beach towels or mat.
- Snorkeling gear (if you have yours).
- Waterproof phone case or pouch.
- Beach bag.

5. Toiletries and Personal Care:
- Travel-sized toiletries (shampoo, conditioner, body wash etc).
- Toothbrush, toothpaste, and floss.
- Medications or any vital prescriptions.
- Insect repellents.

6. Miscellaneous:
- Cash and credit/debit cards.
- Reusable water bottle to stay hydrated.
- Pocket umbrella or rain coats.
- This guide book.
- Entertainment items like books, travel games, mp3 player.

Do well to pack according to specific activities you have planned down, and make sure to pack lightly too, if possible.

CONCLUSION

Thank you for joining us on this interesting adventure across the Cayman Islands. We hope you've enjoyed experiencing the rich culture, breathtaking scenery, scrumptious food, and thrilling activities that this Caribbean paradise has to offer. It has been our pleasure to be your virtual guide and present you with detailed information, exclusive advice, and interactive experiences.

We thank you for concluding our travel guide, and we hope it has been a beneficial resource in arranging your vacation to the Cayman Islands. Now that you have all the facts at your fingertips, we invite you to start on your voyage and make wonderful memories.

As you visit the islands, we would love to hear about your experiences. Share your tales, images, and suggestions with friends and other travelers. Your views may inspire and encourage others on their own Cayman Islands trip.

We respectfully seek your help by giving good and constructive reviews and comments on sites like Amazon. Your opinion is crucial in helping us improve and continue publishing high-quality travel guides that cater to the requirements of dedicated travelers like yourself.

Once again, we express our thanks for picking our guide to traverse the beauties of the Cayman Islands. If you're hungry for more travel inspiration, be sure to check out other travel guides in our series. And don't forget to follow our author page for details on new titles and fascinating trips.

Wishing you a fantastic voyage filled with learning, leisure, and treasured moments. Safe travels, and may your stay in the Cayman Islands be wonderful!

About the Author

Christine M. Edmonson is an ardent traveler, writer, and explorer of the world's hidden jewels. With a love for exploring the unique features of each trip, Christine has committed herself to share her experiences and expertise via travel guides.

With a strong eye for detail and a gift for storytelling, Christine brings the colorful fabric of the Cayman Islands to life in her travel guide. Her objective is to present readers with thorough and fascinating information that enriches their travel experiences and helps them to completely immerse themselves in the area.

Christine believes in the transforming power of travel and its potential to extend perspectives, enhance cultural understanding, and create lifetime experiences. Through her work, she seeks to inspire and motivate readers to go on their own unique experiences.

Stay connected with Christine M. Edmonson and be the first to hear about her new publications by following her author page on Amazon. Join her on a voyage of exploration and let her lead you to remarkable sites throughout the world.

To contact Christine or share your travel stories, feel free to reach out to her at:
Facebook: Christine M. Edmonson
edmonsonchristine@gmail.com

Printed in Great Britain
by Amazon

35664111R00126